C000108484

DERIVATIVES WORKBOOK

CFA Institute is the premier association for investment professionals around the world, with over 142,000 members in 159 countries. Since 1963 the organization has developed and administered the renowned Chartered Financial Analyst® Program. With a rich history of leading the investment profession, CFA Institute has set the highest standards in ethics, education, and professional excellence within the global investment community, and is the foremost authority on investment profession conduct and practice. Each book in the CFA Institute Investment Series is geared toward industry practitioners along with graduate-level finance students and covers the most important topics in the industry. The authors of these cutting-edge books are themselves industry professionals and academics and bring their wealth of knowledge and expertise to this series.

DERIVATIVES WORKBOOK

Wendy L. Pirie, CFA

WILEY

Cover image: © AvDe/Shutterstock
Cover design: Wiley

Copyright © 2017 by CFA Institute. All rights reserved.

Published by John Wiley & Sons, Inc., Hoboken, New Jersey.
Published simultaneously in Canada.

No part of this publication may be reproduced, stored in a retrieval system, or transmitted in any form or by any means, electronic, mechanical, photocopying, recording, scanning, or otherwise, except as permitted under Section 107 or 108 of the 1976 United States Copyright Act, without either the prior written permission of the Publisher, or authorization through payment of the appropriate per-copy fee to the Copyright Clearance Center, Inc., 222 Rosewood Drive, Danvers, MA 01923, (978) 750-8400, fax (978) 646-8600, or on the Web at www.copyright.com. Requests to the Publisher for permission should be addressed to the Permissions Department, John Wiley & Sons, Inc., 111 River Street, Hoboken, NJ 07030, (201) 748-6011, fax (201) 748-6008, or online at http://www.wiley.com/go/permissions.

Limit of Liability/Disclaimer of Warranty: While the publisher and author have used their best efforts in preparing this book, they make no representations or warranties with respect to the accuracy or completeness of the contents of this book and specifically disclaim any implied warranties of merchantability or fitness for a particular purpose. No warranty may be created or extended by sales representatives or written sales materials. The advice and strategies contained herein may not be suitable for your situation. You should consult with a professional where appropriate. Neither the publisher nor author shall be liable for any loss of profit or any other commercial damages, including but not limited to special, incidental, consequential, or other damages.

For general information on our other products and services or for technical support, please contact our Customer Care Department within the United States at (800) 762-2974, outside the United States at (317) 572-3993 or fax (317) 572-4002.

Wiley publishes in a variety of print and electronic formats and by print-on-demand. Some material included with standard print versions of this book may not be included in e-books or in print-on-demand. If this book refers to media such as a CD or DVD that is not included in the version you purchased, you may download this material at http://booksupport.wiley.com. For more information about Wiley products, visit www.wiley.com.

ISBN 9781119381839 (Paperback)
ISBN 9781119381907 (ePDF)
ISBN 9781119381785 (ePub)

Printed in the United States of America

10 9 8 7 6 5 4 3 2 1

CONTENTS

DERIVATIVES WORKBOOK

PART I

LEARNING OBJECTIVES, SUMMARY OVERVIEW, AND PROBLEMS

CHAPTER 1

DERIVATIVE MARKETS AND INSTRUMENTS

LEARNING OUTCOMES

After completing this chapter, you will be able to do the following:

- define a derivative and distinguish between exchange-traded and over-the-counter derivatives;
- contrast forward commitments with contingent claims;
- define forward contracts, futures contracts, options (calls and puts), swaps, and credit derivatives and compare their basic characteristics;
- describe purposes of, and controversies related to, derivative markets;
- explain arbitrage and the role it plays in determining prices and promoting market efficiency.

SUMMARY OVERVIEW

This first reading on derivatives introduces you to the basic characteristics of derivatives, including the following points:
- A derivative is a financial instrument that derives its performance from the performance of an underlying asset.
- The underlying asset, called the underlying, trades in the cash or spot markets and its price is called the cash or spot price.
- Derivatives consist of two general classes: forward commitments and contingent claims.
- Derivatives can be created as standardized instruments on derivatives exchanges or as customized instruments in the over-the-counter market.
- Exchange-traded derivatives are standardized, highly regulated, and transparent transactions that are guaranteed against default through the clearinghouse of the derivatives exchange.

- Over-the-counter derivatives are customized, flexible, and more private and less regulated than exchange-traded derivatives, but are subject to a greater risk of default.
- A forward contract is an over-the-counter derivative contract in which two parties agree that one party, the buyer, will purchase an underlying asset from the other party, the seller, at a later date and at a fixed price they agree upon when the contract is signed.
- A futures contract is similar to a forward contract but is a standardized derivative contract created and traded on a futures exchange. In the contract, two parties agree that one party, the buyer, will purchase an underlying asset from the other party, the seller, at a later date and at a price agreed on by the two parties when the contract is initiated. In addition, there is a daily settling of gains and losses and a credit guarantee by the futures exchange through its clearinghouse.
- A swap is an over-the-counter derivative contract in which two parties agree to exchange a series of cash flows whereby one party pays a variable series that will be determined by an underlying asset or rate and the other party pays either a variable series determined by a different underlying asset or rate or a fixed series.
- An option is a derivative contract in which one party, the buyer, pays a sum of money to the other party, the seller or writer, and receives the right to either buy or sell an underlying asset at a fixed price either on a specific expiration date or at any time prior to the expiration date.
- A call is an option that provides the right to buy the underlying.
- A put is an option that provides the right to sell the underlying.
- Credit derivatives are a class of derivative contracts between two parties, the credit protection buyer and the credit protection seller, in which the latter provides protection to the former against a specific credit loss.
- A credit default swap is the most widely used credit derivative. It is a derivative contract between two parties, a credit protection buyer and a credit protection seller, in which the buyer makes a series of payments to the seller and receives a promise of compensation for credit losses resulting from the default of a third party.
- An asset-backed security is a derivative contract in which a portfolio of debt instruments is assembled and claims are issued on the portfolio in the form of tranches, which have different priorities of claims on the payments made by the debt securities such that prepayments or credit losses are allocated to the most-junior tranches first and the most-senior tranches last.
- Derivatives can be combined with other derivatives or underlying assets to form hybrids.
- Derivatives are issued on equities, fixed-income securities, interest rates, currencies, commodities, credit, and a variety of such diverse underlyings as weather, electricity, and disaster claims.
- Derivatives facilitate the transfer of risk, enable the creation of strategies and payoffs not otherwise possible with spot assets, provide information about the spot market, offer lower transaction costs, reduce the amount of capital required, are easier than the underlyings to go short, and improve the efficiency of spot markets.
- Derivatives are sometimes criticized for being a form of legalized gambling and for leading to destabilizing speculation, although these points can generally be refuted.
- Derivatives are typically priced by forming a hedge involving the underlying asset and a derivative such that the combination must pay the risk-free rate and do so for only one derivative price.
- Derivatives pricing relies heavily on the principle of storage, meaning the ability to hold or store the underlying asset. Storage can incur costs but can also generate cash, such as dividends and interest.

- Arbitrage is the condition that two equivalent assets or derivatives or combinations of assets and derivatives sell for different prices, leading to an opportunity to buy at the low price and sell at the high price, thereby earning a risk-free profit without committing any capital.
- The combined actions of arbitrageurs bring about a convergence of prices. Hence, arbitrage leads to the law of one price: Transactions that produce equivalent results must sell for equivalent prices.

PROBLEMS

1. A derivative is *best* described as a financial instrument that derives its performance by:
   A. passing through the returns of the underlying.
   B. replicating the performance of the underlying.
   C. transforming the performance of the underlying.
2. Compared with exchange-traded derivatives, over-the-counter derivatives would *most likely* be described as:
   A. standardized.
   B. less transparent.
   C. more transparent.
3. Exchange-traded derivatives are:
   A. largely unregulated.
   B. traded through an informal network.
   C. guaranteed by a clearinghouse against default.
4. Which of the following derivatives is classified as a contingent claim?
   A. Futures contracts
   B. Interest rate swaps
   C. Credit default swaps
5. In contrast to contingent claims, forward commitments provide the:
   A. right to buy or sell the underlying asset in the future.
   B. obligation to buy or sell the underlying asset in the future.
   C. promise to provide credit protection in the event of default.
6. Which of the following derivatives provide payoffs that are non-linearly related to the payoffs of the underlying?
   A. Options
   B. Forwards
   C. Interest rate swaps
7. An interest rate swap is a derivative contract in which:
   A. two parties agree to exchange a series of cash flows.
   B. the credit seller provides protection to the credit buyer.
   C. the buyer has the right to purchase the underlying from the seller.
8. Forward commitments subject to default are:
   A. forwards and futures.
   B. futures and interest rate swaps.
   C. interest rate swaps and forwards.

© 2013 CFA Institute. All rights reserved.

9. Which of the following derivatives is *least likely* to have a value of zero at initiation of the contract?
   A. Futures
   B. Options
   C. Forwards
10. A credit derivative is a derivative contract in which the:
   A. clearinghouse provides a credit guarantee to both the buyer and the seller.
   B. seller provides protection to the buyer against the credit risk of a third party.
   C. the buyer and seller provide a performance bond at initiation of the contract.
11. Compared with the underlying spot market, derivative markets are *more likely* to have:
   A. greater liquidity.
   B. higher transaction costs.
   C. higher capital requirements.
12. Which of the following characteristics is *least likely* to be a benefit associated with using derivatives?
   A. More effective management of risk
   B. Payoffs similar to those associated with the underlying
   C. Greater opportunities to go short compared with the spot market
13. Which of the following is *most likely* to be a destabilizing consequence of speculation using derivatives?
   A. Increased defaults by speculators and creditors
   B. Market price swings resulting from arbitrage activities
   C. The creation of trading strategies that result in asymmetric performance
14. The law of one price is *best* described as:
   A. the true fundamental value of an asset.
   B. earning a risk-free profit without committing any capital.
   C. two assets that will produce the same cash flows in the future must sell for equivalent prices.
15. Arbitrage opportunities exist when:
   A. two identical assets or derivatives sell for different prices.
   B. combinations of the underlying asset and a derivative earn the risk-free rate.
   C. arbitrageurs simultaneously buy takeover targets and sell takeover acquirers.

CHAPTER 2

BASICS OF DERIVATIVE PRICING AND VALUATION

LEARNING OUTCOMES

After completing this chapter, you will be able to do the following:

- explain how the concepts of arbitrage, replication, and risk neutrality are used in pricing derivatives;
- distinguish between value and price of forward and futures contracts;
- explain how the value and price of a forward contract are determined at expiration, during the life of the contract, and at initiation;
- describe monetary and nonmonetary benefits and costs associated with holding the underlying asset and explain how they affect the value and price of a forward contract;
- define a forward rate agreement and describe its uses;
- explain why forward and futures prices differ;
- explain how swap contracts are similar to but different from a series of forward contracts;
- distinguish between the value and price of swaps;
- explain how the value of a European option is determined at expiration;
- explain the exercise value, time value, and moneyness of an option;
- identify the factors that determine the value of an option and explain how each factor affects the value of an option;
- explain put–call parity for European options;
- explain put–call–forward parity for European options;
- explain how the value of an option is determined using a one-period binomial model;
- explain under which circumstances the values of European and American options differ.

SUMMARY OVERVIEW

This reading on derivative pricing provides a foundation for understanding how derivatives are valued and traded. Key points include the following:

- The price of the underlying asset is equal to the expected future price discounted at the risk-free rate, plus a risk premium, plus the present value of any benefits, minus the present value of any costs associated with holding the asset.
- An arbitrage opportunity occurs when two identical assets or combinations of assets sell at different prices, leading to the possibility of buying the cheaper asset and selling the more expensive asset to produce a risk-free return without investing any capital.
- In well-functioning markets, arbitrage opportunities are quickly exploited, and the resulting increased buying of underpriced assets and increased selling of overpriced assets returns prices to equivalence.
- Derivatives are priced by creating a risk-free combination of the underlying and a derivative, leading to a unique derivative price that eliminates any possibility of arbitrage.
- Derivative pricing through arbitrage precludes any need for determining risk premiums or the risk aversion of the party trading the option and is referred to as risk-neutral pricing.
- The value of a forward contract at expiration is the value of the asset minus the forward price.
- The value of a forward contract prior to expiration is the value of the asset minus the present value of the forward price.
- The forward price, established when the contract is initiated, is the price agreed to by the two parties that produces a zero value at the start.
- Costs incurred and benefits received by holding the underlying affect the forward price by raising and lowering it, respectively.
- Futures prices can differ from forward prices because of the effect of interest rates on the interim cash flows from the daily settlement.
- Swaps can be priced as an implicit series of off-market forward contracts, whereby each contract is priced the same, resulting in some contracts being positively valued and some negatively valued but with their combined value equaling zero.
- At expiration, a European call or put is worth its exercise value, which for calls is the greater of zero or the underlying price minus the exercise price and for puts is the greater of zero and the exercise price minus the underlying price.
- European calls and puts are affected by the value of the underlying, the exercise price, the risk-free rate, the time to expiration, the volatility of the underlying, and any costs incurred or benefits received while holding the underlying.
- Option values experience time value decay, which is the loss in value due to the passage of time and the approach of expiration, plus the moneyness and the volatility.
- The minimum value of a European call is the maximum of zero and the underlying price minus the present value of the exercise price.
- The minimum value of a European put is the maximum of zero and the present value of the exercise price minus the price of the underlying.
- European put and call prices are related through put–call parity, which specifies that the put price plus the price of the underlying equals the call price plus the present value of the exercise price.
- European put and call prices are related through put–call–forward parity, which shows that the put price plus the value of a risk-free bond with face value equal to the forward price

equals the call price plus the value of a risk-free bond with face value equal to the exercise price.
- The values of European options can be obtained using the binomial model, which specifies two possible prices of the asset one period later and enables the construction of a risk-free hedge consisting of the option and the underlying.
- American call prices can differ from European call prices only if there are cash flows on the underlying, such as dividends or interest; these cash flows are the only reason for early exercise of a call.
- American put prices can differ from European put prices, because the right to exercise early always has value for a put, which is because of a lower limit on the value of the underlying.

PROBLEMS

1. An arbitrage opportunity is *least likely* to be exploited when:
   A. one position is illiquid.
   B. the price differential between assets is large.
   C. the investor can execute a transaction in large volumes.
2. An arbitrageur will *most likely* execute a trade when:
   A. transaction costs are low.
   B. costs of short-selling are high.
   C. prices are consistent with the law of one price.
3. An arbitrage transaction generates a net inflow of funds:
   A. throughout the holding period.
   B. at the end of the holding period.
   C. at the start of the holding period.
4. The price of a forward contract:
   A. is the amount paid at initiation.
   B. is the amount paid at expiration.
   C. fluctuates over the term of the contract.
5. Assume an asset pays no dividends or interest, and also assume that the asset does not yield any non-financial benefits or incur any carrying cost. At initiation, the price of a forward contract on that asset is:
   A. lower than the value of the contract.
   B. equal to the value of the contract.
   C. greater than the value of the contract.
6. With respect to a forward contract, as market conditions change:
   A. only the price fluctuates.
   B. only the value fluctuates.
   C. both the price and the value fluctuate.
7. The value of a forward contract at expiration is:
   A. positive to the long party if the spot price is higher than the forward price.
   B. negative to the short party if the forward price is higher than the spot price.
   C. positive to the short party if the spot price is higher than the forward price.

© 2014 CFA Institute. All rights reserved.

8. At the initiation of a forward contract on an asset that neither receives benefits nor incurs carrying costs during the term of the contract, the forward price is equal to the:
   A. spot price.
   B. future value of the spot price.
   C. present value of the spot price.

9. Stocks BWQ and ZER are each currently priced at $100 per share. Over the next year, stock BWQ is expected to generate significant benefits whereas stock ZER is not expected to generate any benefits. There are no carrying costs associated with holding either stock over the next year. Compared with ZER, the one-year forward price of BWQ is *most likely*:
   A. lower.
   B. the same.
   C. higher.

10. If the net cost of carry of an asset is positive, then the price of a forward contract on that asset is *most likely*:
    A. lower than if the net cost of carry was zero.
    B. the same as if the net cost of carry was zero.
    C. higher than if the net cost of carry was zero.

11. If the present value of storage costs exceeds the present value of its convenience yield, then the commodity's forward price is *most likely*:
    A. less than the spot price compounded at the risk-free rate.
    B. the same as the spot price compounded at the risk-free rate.
    C. higher than the spot price compounded at the risk-free rate.

12. Which of the following factors *most likely* explains why the spot price of a commodity in short supply can be greater than its forward price?
    A. Opportunity cost
    B. Lack of dividends
    C. Convenience yield

13. When interest rates are constant, futures prices are *most likely*:
    A. less than forward prices.
    B. equal to forward prices.
    C. greater than forward prices.

14. In contrast to a forward contract, a futures contract:
    A. trades over-the-counter.
    B. is initiated at a zero value.
    C. is marked-to-market daily.

15. To the holder of a long position, it is more desirable to own a forward contract than a futures contract when interest rates and futures prices are:
    A. negatively correlated.
    B. uncorrelated.
    C. positively correlated.

16. The value of a swap typically:
    A. is non-zero at initiation.
    B. is obtained through replication.
    C. does not fluctuate over the life of the contract.

17. The price of a swap typically:
    A. is zero at initiation.
    B. fluctuates over the life of the contract.
    C. is obtained through a process of replication.

18. The value of a swap is equal to the present value of the:
    A. fixed payments from the swap.
    B. net cash flow payments from the swap.
    C. underlying at the end of the contract.
19. A European call option and a European put option are written on the same underlying, and both options have the same expiration date and exercise price. At expiration, it is possible that both options will have:
    A. negative values.
    B. the same value.
    C. positive values.
20. At expiration, a European put option will be valuable if the exercise price is:
    A. less than the underlying price.
    B. equal to the underlying price.
    C. greater than the underlying price.
21. The value of a European call option at expiration is the greater of zero or the:
    A. value of the underlying.
    B. value of the underlying minus the exercise price.
    C. exercise price minus the value of the underlying.
22. For a European call option with two months until expiration, if the spot price is below the exercise price, the call option will *most likely* have:
    A. zero time value.
    B. positive time value.
    C. positive exercise value.
23. When the price of the underlying is below the exercise price, a put option is:
    A. in-the-money.
    B. at-the-money.
    C. out-of-the-money.
24. If the risk-free rate increases, the value of an in-the-money European put option will *most likely*:
    A. decrease.
    B. remain the same.
    C. increase.
25. The value of a European call option is inversely related to the:
    A. exercise price.
    B. time to expiration.
    C. volatility of the underlying.
26. The table below shows three European call options on the same underlying:

	Time to Expiration	Exercise Price
Option 1	3 months	$100
Option 2	6 months	$100
Option 3	6 months	$105

The option with the highest value is *most likely*:
    A. Option 1.
    B. Option 2.
    C. Option 3.

27. The value of a European put option can be either directly or inversely related to the:
    A. exercise price.
    B. time to expiration.
    C. volatility of the underlying.

28. Prior to expiration, the lowest value of a European put option is the greater of zero or the:
    A. exercise price minus the value of the underlying.
    B. present value of the exercise price minus the value of the underlying.
    C. value of the underlying minus the present value of the exercise price.

29. A European put option on a dividend-paying stock is *most likely* to increase if there is an increase in:
    A. carrying costs.
    B. the risk-free rate.
    C. dividend payments.

30. Based on put-call parity, a trader who combines a long asset, a long put, and a short call will create a synthetic:
    A. long bond.
    B. fiduciary call.
    C. protective put.

31. Which of the following transactions is the equivalent of a synthetic long call position?
    A. Long asset, long put, short call
    B. Long asset, long put, short bond
    C. Short asset, long call, long bond

32. Which of the following is *least likely* to be required by the binomial option pricing model?
    A. Spot price
    B. Two possible prices one period later
    C. Actual probabilities of the up and down moves

33. An at-the-money American call option on a stock that pays no dividends has three months remaining until expiration. The market value of the option will *most likely* be:
    A. less than its exercise value.
    B. equal to its exercise value.
    C. greater than its exercise value.

34. At expiration, American call options are worth:
    A. less than European call options.
    B. the same as European call options.
    C. more than European call options.

35. Which of the following circumstances will *most likely* affect the value of an American call option relative to a European call option?
    A. Dividends are declared
    B. Expiration date occurs
    C. The risk-free rate changes

36. Combining a protective put with a forward contract generates equivalent outcomes at expiration to those of a:
    A. fiduciary call.
    B. long call combined with a short asset.
    C. forward contract combined with a risk-free bond.

CHAPTER 3

PRICING AND VALUATION OF FORWARD COMMITMENTS

LEARNING OUTCOMES

After completing this chapter, you will be able to do the following:

- describe and compare how equity, interest rate, fixed-income, and currency forward and futures contracts are priced and valued;
- calculate and interpret the no-arbitrage value of equity, interest rate, fixed-income, and currency forward and futures contracts;
- describe and compare how interest rate, currency, and equity swaps are priced and valued;
- calculate and interpret the no-arbitrage value of interest rate, currency, and equity swaps.

SUMMARY OVERVIEW

This reading on forward commitment pricing and valuation provides a foundation for understanding how forwards, futures, and swaps are both priced and valued.

Key points include the following:

- The arbitrageur would rather have more money than less and abides by two fundamental rules: Do not use your own money, and do not take any price risk.
- The no-arbitrage approach is used for the pricing and valuation of forward commitments and is built on the key concept of the law of one price, which states that if two investments have the same future cash flows, regardless of what happens in the future, these two investments should have the same current price.
- Throughout this reading, the following key assumptions are made:
  - Replicating instruments are identifiable and investable.
  - Market frictions are nil.
  - Short selling is allowed with full use of proceeds.
  - Borrowing and lending is available at a known risk-free rate.

- Carry arbitrage models used for forward commitment pricing and valuation are based on the no-arbitrage approach.
- With forward commitments, there is a distinct difference between pricing and valuation; pricing involves the determination of the appropriate fixed price or rate, and valuation involves the determination of the contract's current value expressed in currency units.
- Forward commitment pricing results in determining a price or rate such that the forward contract value is equal to zero.
- The price of a forward commitment is a function of the price of the underlying instrument, financing costs, and other carry costs and benefits.
- With equities, currencies, and fixed-income securities, the forward price is determined such that the initial forward value is zero.
- With forward rate agreements, the fixed interest rate is determined such that the initial value of the FRA is zero.
- Futures contract pricing here can essentially be treated the same as forward contract pricing.
- Because of daily marking to market, futures contract values are zero after each daily settlement.
- The general approach to pricing and valuing swaps as covered here is using a replicating or hedge portfolio of comparable instruments.
- With a basic understanding of pricing and valuing a simple interest rate swap, it is a straightforward extension to pricing and valuing currency swaps and equity swaps.
- With interest rate swaps and some equity swaps, pricing involves solving for the fixed interest rate.
- With currency swaps, pricing involves solving for the two fixed rates as well as the notional amounts in each currency.

PROBLEMS

The following information relates to Questions 1–7

Donald Troubadour is a derivatives trader for Southern Shores Investments. The firm seeks arbitrage opportunities in the forward and futures markets using the carry arbitrage model.

Troubadour identifies an arbitrage opportunity relating to a fixed-income futures contract and its underlying bond. Current data on the futures contract and underlying bond are presented in Exhibit 1. The current annual compounded risk-free rate is 0.30%.

EXHIBIT 1   Current Data for Futures and Underlying Bond

Futures Contract		Underlying Bond	
Quoted futures price	125.00	Quoted bond price	112.00
Conversion factor	0.90	Accrued interest since last coupon payment	0.08
Time remaining to contract expiration	Three months	Accrued interest at futures contract expiration	0.20
Accrued interest over life of futures contract	0.00		

© 2016 CFA Institute. All rights reserved.

Troubadour next gathers information on three existing positions.

Position 1 (Nikkei 225 Futures Contract):

Troubadour holds a long position in a Nikkei 225 futures contract that has a remaining maturity of three months. The continuously compounded dividend yield on the Nikkei 225 Stock Index is 1.1%, and the current stock index level is 16,080. The continuously compounded annual interest rate is 0.2996%.

Position 2 (Euro/JGB Forward Contract):

One month ago, Troubadour purchased euro/yen forward contracts with three months to expiration at a quoted price of 100.20 (quoted as a percentage of par). The contract notional amount is ¥100,000,000. The current forward price is 100.05.

Position 3 (JPY/USD Currency Forward Contract):

Troubadour holds a short position in a yen/US dollar forward contract with a notional value of $1,000,000. At contract initiation, the forward rate was ¥112.10 per $1. The forward contract expires in three months. The current spot exchange rate is ¥112.00 per $1, and the annually compounded risk-free rates are –0.20% for the yen and 0.30% for the US dollar. The current quoted price of the forward contract is equal to the no-arbitrage price.

Troubadour next considers an equity forward contract for Texas Steel, Inc. (TSI). Information regarding TSI common shares and a TSI equity forward contract is presented in Exhibit 2.

EXHIBIT 2   Selected Information for TSI

- TSI has historically paid dividends every six months.
- The price per share of TSI's common shares is $250.
- The forward price per share for a nine-month TSI equity forward contract is $250.562289.
- Assume annual compounding.

Troubadour takes a short position in the TSI equity forward contract. His supervisor asks, "Under which scenario would our position experience a loss?"

Three months after contract initiation, Troubadour gathers information on TSI and the risk-free rate, which is presented in Exhibit 3.

EXHIBIT 3   Selected Data on TSI and the Risk-Free Rate

- The price per share of TSI's common shares is $245.
- The risk-free rate is 0.325% (quoted on an annual compounding basis).
- TSI recently announced its regular semiannual dividend of $1.50 per share that will be paid exactly three months before contract expiration.
- The market price of the TSI equity forward contract is equal to the no-arbitrage forward price.

1. Based on Exhibit 2 and assuming annual compounding, the arbitrage profit on the bond futures contract is *closest* to:
   A. 0.4158.
   B. 0.5356.
   C. 0.6195.
2. The current no-arbitrage futures price of the Nikkei 225 futures contract (Position 1) is *closest* to:
   A. 15,951.81.
   B. 16,047.86.
   C. 16,112.21.
3. The value of Position 2 is *closest* to:
   A. −¥149,925.
   B. −¥150,000.
   C. −¥150,075.
4. The value of Position 3 is *closest* to:
   A. −¥40,020.
   B. ¥139,913.
   C. ¥239,963.
5. Based on Exhibit 2, Troubadour should find that an arbitrage opportunity relating to TSI shares is
   A. not available.
   B. available based on carry arbitrage.
   C. available based on reverse carry arbitrage.
6. The *most appropriate* response to Troubadour's supervisor's question regarding the TSI forward contract is:
   A. a decrease in TSI's share price, all else equal.
   B. an increase in the risk-free rate, all else equal
   C. a decrease in the market price of the forward contract, all else equal.
7. Based on Exhibits 2 and 3, and assuming annual compounding, the per share value of Troubadour's short position in the TSI forward contract three months after contract initiation is *closest* to:
   A. $1.6549.
   B. $5.1561.
   C. $6.6549.

The following information relates to Questions 8–16

Sonal Johnson is a risk manager for a bank. She manages the bank's risks using a combination of swaps and forward rate agreements (FRAs).

Johnson prices a three-year Libor-based interest rate swap with annual resets using the present value factors presented in Exhibit 1.

EXHIBIT 1   Present Value Factors

Maturity (years)	Present Value Factors
1	0.990099
2	0.977876
3	0.965136

Johnson also uses the present value factors in Exhibit 1 to value an interest rate swap that the bank entered into one year ago as the receive-floating party. Selected data for the swap are presented in Exhibit 2. Johnson notes that the current equilibrium two-year fixed swap rate is 1.00%.

EXHIBIT 2   Selected Data on Fixed for Floating Interest Rate Swap

Swap notional amount	$50,000,000
Original swap term	Three years, with annual resets
Fixed swap rate (since initiation)	3.00%

One of the bank's investments is exposed to movements in the Japanese yen, and Johnson desires to hedge the currency exposure. She prices a one-year fixed-for-fixed currency swap involving yen and US dollars, with a quarterly reset. Johnson uses the interest rate data presented in Exhibit 3 to price the currency swap.

EXHIBIT 3   Selected Japanese and US Interest Rate Data

Days to Maturity	Yen Spot Interest Rates	US Dollar Spot Interest Rates
90	0.05%	0.20%
180	0.10%	0.40%
270	0.15%	0.55%
360	0.25%	0.70%

Johnson next reviews an equity swap with an annual reset that the bank entered into six months ago as the receive-fixed, pay-equity party. Selected data regarding the equity swap, which is linked to an equity index, are presented in Exhibit 4. At the time of initiation, the underlying equity index was trading at 100.00.

EXHIBIT 4   Selected Data on Equity Swap

Swap notional amount	$20,000,000
Original swap term	Five years, with annual resets
Fixed swap rate	2.00%

The equity index is currently trading at 103.00, and relevant US spot rates, along with their associated present value factors, are presented in Exhibit 5.

EXHIBIT 5   Selected US Spot Rates and Present Value Factors

Maturity (years)	Spot Rate	Present Value Factors
0.5	0.40%	0.998004
1.5	1.00%	0.985222
2.5	1.20%	0.970874
3.5	2.00%	0.934579
4.5	2.60%	0.895255

Johnson reviews a 6 × 9 FRA that the bank entered into 90 days ago as the pay-fixed/receive-floating party. Selected data for the FRA are presented in Exhibit 6, and current Libor data are presented in Exhibit 7. Based on her interest rate forecast, Johnson also considers whether the bank should enter into new positions in 1 × 4 and 2 × 5 FRAs.

EXHIBIT 6   6 × 9 FRA Data

FRA term	6 × 9
FRA rate	0.70%
FRA notional amount	US$20,000,000
FRA settlement terms	Advanced set, advanced settle

EXHIBIT 7   Current Libor

30-day Libor	0.75%
60-day Libor	0.82%
90-day Libor	0.90%
120-day Libor	0.92%
150-day Libor	0.94%
180-day Libor	0.95%
210-day Libor	0.97%
270-day Libor	1.00%

Three months later, the 6 × 9 FRA in Exhibit 6 reaches expiration, at which time the three-month US dollar Libor is 1.10% and the six-month US dollar Libor is 1.20%. Johnson determines that the appropriate discount rate for the FRA settlement cash flows is 1.10%.

8. Based on Exhibit 1, Johnson should price the three-year Libor-based interest rate swap at a fixed rate *closest* to:
   A. 0.34%.
   B. 1.16%.
   C. 1.19%.
9. From the bank's perspective, using data from Exhibit 1, the current value of the swap described in Exhibit 2 is *closest* to:
   A. −$2,951,963.
   B. −$1,967,975.
   C. −$1,943,000.
10. Based on Exhibit 3, Johnson should determine that the annualized equilibrium fixed swap rate for Japanese yen is *closest* to:
    A. 0.0624%.
    B. 0.1375%.
    C. 0.2496%.

11. From the bank's perspective, using data from Exhibits 4 and 5, the fair value of the equity swap is *closest* to:
    A. −$1,139,425.
    B. −$781,323.
    C. −$181,323.

12. Based on Exhibit 5, the current value of the equity swap described in Exhibit 4 would be zero if the equity index was currently trading the *closest* to:
    A. 97.30.
    B. 99.09.
    C. 100.00.

13. From the bank's perspective, based on Exhibits 6 and 7, the value of the 6 × 9 FRA 90 days after inception is *closest* to:
    A. $14,817.
    B. $19,647.
    C. $29,635.

14. Based on Exhibit 7, the no-arbitrage fixed rate on a new 1 × 4 FRA is *closest* to:
    A. 0.65%.
    B. 0.73%.
    C. 0.98%.

15. Based on Exhibit 7, the fixed rate on a new 2 × 5 FRA is *closest* to:
    A. 0.61%.
    B. 1.02%.
    C. 1.71%.

16. Based on Exhibit 6 and the three-month US dollar Libor at expiration, the payment amount that the bank will receive to settle the 6 × 9 FRA is *closest* to:
    A. $19,945.
    B. $24,925.
    C. $39,781.

CHAPTER 4

VALUATION OF CONTINGENT CLAIMS

LEARNING OUTCOMES

After completing this chapter, you will be able to do the following:

- describe and interpret the binomial option valuation model and its component terms;
- calculate the no-arbitrage values of European and American options using a two-period binomial model;
- identify an arbitrage opportunity involving options and describe the related arbitrage;
- describe how interest rate options are valued using a two-period binomial model;
- calculate and interpret the value of an interest rate option using a two-period binomial model;
- describe how the value of a European option can be analyzed as the present value of the option's expected payoff at expiration;
- identify assumptions of the Black–Scholes–Merton option valuation model;
- interpret the components of the Black–Scholes–Merton model as applied to call options in terms of a leveraged position in the underlying;
- describe how the Black–Scholes–Merton model is used to value European options on equities and currencies;
- describe how the Black model is used to value European options on futures;
- describe how the Black model is used to value European interest rate options and European swaptions;
- interpret each of the option Greeks;
- describe how a delta hedge is executed;
- describe the role of gamma risk in options trading;
- define implied volatility and explain how it is used in options trading.

SUMMARY OVERVIEW

This reading on the valuation of contingent claims provides a foundation for understanding how a variety of different options are valued. Key points include the following:

- The arbitrageur would rather have more money than less and abides by two fundamental rules: Do not use your own money and do not take any price risk.
- The no-arbitrage approach is used for option valuation and is built on the key concept of the law of one price, which says that if two investments have the same future cash flows regardless of what happens in the future, then these two investments should have the same current price.
- Throughout this reading, the following key assumptions are made:
  - Replicating instruments are identifiable and investable.
  - Market frictions are nil.
  - Short selling is allowed with full use of proceeds.
  - The underlying instrument price follows a known distribution.
  - Borrowing and lending is available at a known risk-free rate.
- The two-period binomial model can be viewed as three one-period binomial models, one positioned at Time 0 and two positioned at Time 1.
- In general, European-style options can be valued based on the expectations approach in which the option value is determined as the present value of the expected future option payouts, where the discount rate is the risk-free rate and the expectation is taken based on the risk-neutral probability measure.
- Both American-style options and European-style options can be valued based on the no-arbitrage approach, which provides clear interpretations of the component terms; the option value is determined by working backward through the binomial tree to arrive at the correct current value.
- For American-style options, early exercise influences the option values and hedge ratios as one works backward through the binomial tree.
- Interest rate option valuation requires the specification of an entire term structure of interest rates, so valuation is often estimated via a binomial tree.
- A key assumption of the Black–Scholes–Merton option valuation model is that the return of the underlying instrument follows geometric Brownian motion, implying a lognormal distribution of the return.
- The BSM model can be interpreted as a dynamically managed portfolio of the underlying instrument and zero-coupon bonds.
- BSM model interpretations related to $N(d_1)$ are that it is the basis for the number of units of underlying instrument to replicate an option, that it is the primary determinant of delta, and that it answers the question of how much the option value will change for a small change in the underlying.
- BSM model interpretations related to $N(d_2)$ are that it is the basis for the number of zero-coupon bonds to acquire to replicate an option and that it is the basis for estimating the risk-neutral probability of an option expiring in the money.
- The Black futures option model assumes the underlying is a futures or a forward contract.
- Interest rate options can be valued based on a modified Black futures option model in which the underlying is a forward rate agreement (FRA), there is an accrual period adjustment as well as an underlying notional amount, and that care must be given to day-count conventions.

- An interest rate cap is a portfolio of interest rate call options termed caplets, each with the same exercise rate and with sequential maturities.
- An interest rate floor is a portfolio of interest rate put options termed floorlets, each with the same exercise rate and with sequential maturities.
- A swaption is an option on a swap.
- A payer swaption is an option on a swap to pay fixed and receive floating.
- A receiver swaption is an option on a swap to receive fixed and pay floating.
- Long a callable fixed-rate bond can be viewed as long a straight fixed-rate bond and short a receiver swaption.
- Delta is a static risk measure defined as the change in a given portfolio for a given small change in the value of the underlying instrument, holding everything else constant.
- Delta hedging refers to managing the portfolio delta by entering additional positions into the portfolio.
- A delta neutral portfolio is one in which the portfolio delta is set and maintained at zero.
- A change in the option price can be estimated with a delta approximation.
- Because delta is used to make a linear approximation of the non-linear relationship that exists between the option price and the underlying price, there is an error that can be estimated by gamma.
- Gamma is a static risk measure defined as the change in a given portfolio delta for a given small change in the value of the underlying instrument, holding everything else constant.
- Gamma captures the non-linearity risk or the risk—via exposure to the underlying—that remains once the portfolio is delta neutral.
- A gamma neutral portfolio is one in which the portfolio gamma is maintained at zero.
- The change in the option price can be better estimated by a delta-plus-gamma approximation compared with just a delta approximation.
- Theta is a static risk measure defined as the change in the value of an option given a small change in calendar time, holding everything else constant.
- Vega is a static risk measure defined as the change in a given portfolio for a given small change in volatility, holding everything else constant.
- Rho is a static risk measure defined as the change in a given portfolio for a given small change in the risk-free interest rate, holding everything else constant.
- Although historical volatility can be estimated, there is no objective measure of future volatility.
- Implied volatility is the BSM model volatility that yields the market option price.
- Implied volatility is a measure of future volatility, whereas historical volatility is a measure of past volatility.
- Option prices reflect the beliefs of option market participant about the future volatility of the underlying.
- The volatility smile is a two dimensional plot of the implied volatility with respect to the exercise price.
- The volatility surface is a three dimensional plot of the implied volatility with respect to both expiration time and exercise prices.
- If the BSM model assumptions were true, then one would expect to find the volatility surface flat, but in practice, the volatility surface is not flat.

PROBLEMS

The following information relates to Questions 1–9

Bruno Sousa has been hired recently to work with senior analyst Camila Rocha. Rocha gives him three option valuation tasks.

Alpha Company

Sousa's first task is to illustrate how to value a call option on Alpha Company with a one-period binomial option pricing model. It is a non-dividend-paying stock, and the inputs are as follows.

- The current stock price is 50, and the call option exercise price is 50.
- In one period, the stock price will either rise to 56 or decline to 46.
- The risk-free rate of return is 5% per period.

Based on the model, Rocha asks Sousa to estimate the hedge ratio, the risk-neutral probability of an up move, and the price of the call option. In the illustration, Sousa is also asked to describe related arbitrage positions to use if the call option is overpriced relative to the model.

Beta Company

Next, Sousa uses the two-period binomial model to estimate the value of a European-style call option on Beta Company's common shares. The inputs are as follows.

- The current stock price is 38, and the call option exercise price is 40.
- The up factor (u) is 1.300, and the down factor (d) is 0.800.
- The risk-free rate of return is 3% per period.

Sousa then analyzes a put option on the same stock. All of the inputs, including the exercise price, are the same as for the call option. He estimates that the value of a European-style put option is 4.53. Exhibit 1 summarizes his analysis. Sousa next must determine whether an American-style put option would have the same value.

© 2016 CFA Institute. All rights reserved.

EXHIBIT 1   Two-Period Binomial European-Style Put Option on Beta Company

Item	Value
Underlying	64.22
Put	0

Item	Value
Underlying	49.4
Put	0.2517
Hedge Ratio	−0.01943

Item	Value
Underlying	38
Put	4.5346
Hedge Ratio	−0.4307

Item	Value
Underlying	39.52
Put	0.48

Item	Value
Underlying	30.4
Put	8.4350
Hedge Ratio	−1

Item	Value
Underlying	24.32
Put	15.68

Time = 0   Time = 1   Time = 2

Sousa makes two statements with regard to the valuation of a European-style option under the expectations approach.

Statement 1   The calculation involves discounting at the risk-free rate.
Statement 2   The calculation uses risk-neutral probabilities instead of true probabilities.

Rocha asks Sousa whether it is ever profitable to exercise American options prior to maturity. Sousa answers, "I can think of two possible cases. The first case is the early exercise of an American call option on a dividend-paying stock. The second case is the early exercise of an American put option."

Interest Rate Option

The final option valuation task involves an interest rate option. Sousa must value a two-year, European-style call option on a one-year spot rate. The notional value of the option is 1 million, and the exercise rate is 2.75%. The risk-neutral probability of an up move is 0.50. The current and expected one-year interest rates are shown in Exhibit 2, along with the values of a one-year zero-coupon bond of 1 notional value for each interest rate.

EXHIBIT 2   Two-Year Interest Rate Lattice for an Interest Rate Option

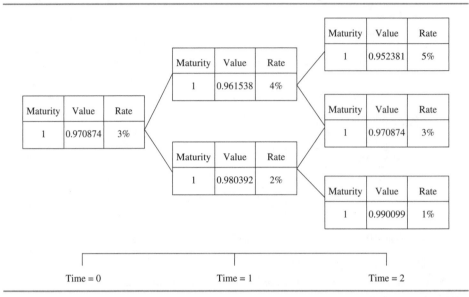

Rocha asks Sousa why the value of a similar in-the-money interest rate call option decreases if the exercise price is higher. Sousa provides two reasons.

Reason 1   The exercise value of the call option is lower.
Reason 2   The risk-neutral probabilities are changed.

1. The optimal hedge ratio for the Alpha Company call option using the one-period binomial model is *closest* to:
   A. 0.60.
   B. 0.67.
   C. 1.67.
2. The risk-neutral probability of the up move for the Alpha Company stock is *closest* to:
   A. 0.06.
   B. 0.40.
   C. 0.65.
3. The value of the Alpha Company call option is *closest* to:
   A. 3.71.
   B. 5.71.
   C. 6.19.
4. For the Alpha Company option, the positions to take advantage of the arbitrage opportunity are to write the call and:
   A. short shares of Alpha stock and lend.
   B. buy shares of Alpha stock and borrow.
   C. short shares of Alpha stock and borrow.

5. The value of the European-style call option on Beta Company shares is *closest* to:
   A. 4.83.
   B. 5.12.
   C. 7.61.
6. The value of the American-style put option on Beta Company shares is *closest* to:
   A. 4.53.
   B. 5.15.
   C. 9.32.
7. Which of Sousa's statements about binomial models is correct?
   A. Statement 1 only
   B. Statement 2 only
   C. Both Statement 1 and Statement 2
8. Based on Exhibit 2 and the parameters used by Sousa, the value of the interest rate option is *closest* to:
   A. 5,251.
   B. 6,236.
   C. 6,429.
9. Which of Sousa's reasons for the decrease in the value of the interest rate option is correct?
   A. Reason 1 only
   B. Reason 2 only
   C. Both Reason 1 and Reason 2

The following information relates to Questions 10–18

Trident Advisory Group manages assets for high-net-worth individuals and family trusts.

Alice Lee, chief investment officer, is meeting with a client, Noah Solomon, to discuss risk management strategies for his portfolio. Solomon is concerned about recent volatility and has asked Lee to explain options valuation and the use of options in risk management.

Options on Stock

Lee begins: "We use the Black–Scholes–Merton (BSM) model for option valuation. To fully understand the BSM model valuation, one needs to understand the assumptions of the model. These assumptions include normally distributed stock returns, constant volatility of return on the underlying, constant interest rates, and continuous prices." Lee uses the BSM model to price TCB, which is one of Solomon's holdings. Exhibit 1 provides the current stock price (S), exercise price (X), risk-free interest rate (r), volatility (σ), and time to expiration (T) in years as well as selected outputs from the BSM model. TCB does not pay a dividend.

EXHIBIT 1   BSM Model for European Options on TCB

		BSM Inputs		
S	X	r	Σ	T
$57.03	55	0.22%	32%	0.25

		BSM Outputs			
d_1	$N(d_1)$	d_2	$N(d_2)$	BSM Call Price	BSM Put Price
0.3100	0.6217	0.1500	0.5596	$4.695	$2.634

Options on Futures

The Black model valuation and selected outputs for options on another of Solomon's holdings, the GPX 500 Index (GPX), are shown in Exhibit 2. The spot index level for the GPX is 187.95, and the index is assumed to pay a continuous dividend at a rate of 2.2% (δ) over the life of the options being valued, which expire in 0.36 years. A futures contract on the GPX also expiring in 0.36 years is currently priced at 186.73.

EXHIBIT 2   Black Model for European Options on the GPX Index

Black Model Inputs					
GPX Index	X	r	σ	T	δ Yield
187.95	180	0.39%	24%	0.36	2.2%

Black Model Call Value	Black Model Put Value	Market Call Price	Market Put Price
$14.2089	$7.4890	$14.26	$7.20

Option Greeks					
Delta (call)	Delta (put)	Gamma (call or put)	Theta (call) daily	Rho (call) per %	Vega per % (call or put)
0.6232	−0.3689	0.0139	−0.0327	0.3705	0.4231

After reviewing Exhibit 2, Solomon asks Lee which option Greek letter best describes the changes in an option's value as time to expiration declines.

Solomon observes that the market price of the put option in Exhibit 2 is $7.20. Lee responds that she used the historical volatility of the GPX of 24% as an input to the BSM model, and she explains the implications for the implied volatility for the GPX.

Options on Interest Rates

Solomon forecasts the three-month Libor will exceed 0.85% in six months and is considering using options to reduce the risk of rising rates. He asks Lee to value an interest rate call with a strike price of 0.85%. The current three-month Libor is 0.60%, and an FRA for a three-month Libor loan beginning in six months is currently 0.75%.

Hedging Strategy for the Equity Index

Solomon's portfolio currently holds 10,000 shares of an exchange-traded fund (ETF) that tracks the GPX. He is worried the index will decline. He remarks to Lee, "You have told me how the BSM model can provide useful information for reducing the risk of my GPX position." Lee suggests a delta hedge as a strategy to protect against small moves in the GPX Index.

Lee also indicates that a long position in puts could be used to hedge larger moves in the GPX. She notes that although hedging with either puts or calls can result in a delta-neutral position, they would need to consider the resulting gamma.

10. Lee's statement about the assumptions of the BSM model is accurate with regard to:
    A. interest rates but not continuous prices.
    B. continuous prices but not the return distribution.
    C. the stock return distribution but not the volatility.
11. Based on Exhibit 1 and the BSM valuation approach, the initial portfolio required to replicate the long call option payoff is:
    A. long 0.3100 shares of TCB stock and short 0.5596 shares of a zero-coupon bond.
    B. long 0.6217 shares of TCB stock and short 0.1500 shares of a zero-coupon bond.
    C. long 0.6217 shares of TCB stock and short 0.5596 shares of a zero-coupon bond.
12. To determine the long put option value on TCB stock in Exhibit 1, the correct BSM valuation approach is to compute:
    A. 0.4404 times the present value of the exercise price minus 0.6217 times the price of TCB stock.
    B. 0.4404 times the present value of the exercise price minus 0.3783 times the price of TCB stock.
    C. 0.5596 times the present value of the exercise price minus 0.6217 times the price of TCB stock.
13. What are the correct spot value (*S*) and the risk-free rate (*r*) that Lee should use as inputs for the Black model?
    A. 186.73 and 0.39%, respectively
    B. 186.73 and 2.20%, respectively
    C. 187.95 and 2.20%, respectively
14. Which of the following is the correct answer to Solomon's question regarding the option Greek letter?
    A. Vega
    B. Theta
    C. Gamma
15. Based on Solomon's observation about the model price and market price for the put option in Exhibit 2, the implied volatility for the GPX is *most likely*:
    A. less than the historical volatility.
    B. equal to the historical volatility.
    C. greater than the historical volatility.
16. The valuation inputs used by Lee to price a call reflecting Solomon's interest rate views should include an underlying FRA rate of:
    A. 0.60% with six months to expiration.
    B. 0.75% with nine months to expiration.
    C. 0.75% with six months to expiration.
17. The strategy suggested by Lee for hedging small moves in Solomon's ETF position would *most likely* involve:
    A. selling put options.
    B. selling call options.
    C. buying call options.
18. Lee's put-based hedge strategy for Solomon's ETF position would *most likely* result in a portfolio gamma that is:
    A. negative.
    B. neutral.
    C. positive.

CHAPTER 5

DERIVATIVES STRATEGIES

LEARNING OUTCOMES

After completing this chapter, you will be able to do the following:

- describe how interest rate, currency, and equity swaps, futures, and forwards can be used to modify risk and return;
- describe how to replicate an asset by using options and by using cash plus forwards or futures;
- describe the investment objectives, structure, payoff, and risk(s) of a covered call position;
- describe the investment objectives, structure, payoff, and risks(s) of a protective put position;
- calculate and interpret the value at expiration, profit, maximum profit, maximum loss, and breakeven underlying price at expiration for covered calls and protective puts;
- contrast protective put and covered call positions to being long an asset and short a forward on the asset;
- describe the investment objective(s), structure, payoffs, and risks of the following option strategies: bull spread, bear spread, collar, and straddle;
- calculate and interpret the value at expiration, profit, maximum profit, maximum loss, and breakeven underlying price at expiration of the following option strategies: bull spread, bear spread, collar, and straddle;
- describe uses of calendar spreads;
- identify and evaluate appropriate derivatives strategies consistent with given investment objectives.

SUMMARY OVERVIEW

This chapter on derivatives strategies shows a number of ways in which market participants might use derivatives to enhance returns or to reduce risk to better meet portfolio objectives. The following are the key points.

- Interest rate, currency, and equity futures and swaps can be used to modify risk and return by altering the characteristics of the cash flows of an investment portfolio.

- Buying a call and writing a put with the same exercise price creates a synthetic long position.
- A long position plus a short futures position in the same underlying asset creates a synthetic risk-free asset earning the risk-free rate.
- A covered call, in which the holder of a stock writes a call giving someone the right to buy the shares, is one of the most common uses of options by individual investors.
- Covered calls can be used to generate income, to acquire shares at a lower-than-market price, or to exit a position when the shares hit a target price.
- A covered call position has a limited maximum return because of the transfer of the right tail of the return distribution to the option buyer.
- The maximum loss of a covered call position is less than the maximum loss of the underlying shares alone, but the covered call carries the potential for an opportunity loss if the underlying shares rise sharply.
- A protective put is the simultaneous holding of a long stock position and a long put on the same asset. The put provides protection or insurance against a price decline.
- Although the continuous purchase of protective puts is expensive and probably suboptimal, the occasional purchase of a protective put to deal with a bearish short-term outlook can be a reasonable risk-reducing activity.
- The maximum loss with a protective put is limited because the downside risk is transferred to the option writer in exchange for the payment of the option premium.
- With an option spread, an investor buys one option and writes another of the same type. This reduces the position cost but caps the maximum payoff.
- A bull spread is normally constructed by buying a call option and writing another call option with a higher exercise price.
- A bear spread is normally constructed by buying a put option and writing another put option with a lower exercise price.
- With either a bull spread or a bear spread, both the maximum gain and the maximum loss are known and limited.
- A collar is an option position in which the investor is long shares of stock and simultaneously writes a covered call and buys a protective put.
- A calendar spread involves buying a long-dated option and writing a shorter-dated option of the same type with the same exercise price, or vice versa. The primary motivation for such a spread is to take advantage of the faster time decay with the shorter-term option.
- A straddle is an option combination in which the investor buys puts and calls with the same exercise price. The straddle holder typically needs a substantial price movement in the underlying asset in order to make a profit.
- The risk of a derivative product depends on how it is used. Derivatives should always be used in connection with a well-defined investment objective.

PROBLEMS

Aline Nuñes is a junior analyst in the derivatives research division of an international securities firm. Nuñes's supervisor, Cátia Pereira, asks her to conduct an analysis of various options trading strategies relating to shares of three companies: IZD, QWY, and XDF. On 1 February, Nuñes gathers selected option premium data on the companies, which is presented in Exhibit 1.

© 2016 CFA Institute. All rights reserved.

EXHIBIT 1   Share Price and Options Premiums as of 1 February (share prices and option premiums are in euros)

	Share Price	Call Premium	Option Date/Strike	Put Premium
		9.45	April/87.50	1.67
IZD	93.93	2.67	April/95.00	4.49
		1.68	April/97.50	5.78
		4.77	April/24.00	0.35
QWY	28.49	3.96	April/25.00	0.50
		0.32	April/31.00	3.00
		0.23	February/80.00	5.52
XDF	74.98	2.54	April/75.00	3.22
		2.47	December/80.00	9.73

Nuñes considers the following option strategies relating to IZD.

Strategy 1: Constructing a synthetic long put position in IZD
Strategy 2: Buying 100 shares of IZD and writing the April €95.00 strike call option on IZD
Strategy 3: Implementing a covered call position in IZD using the April €97.50 strike option

Nuñes next reviews the following option strategies relating to QWY.

Strategy 4: Implementing a protective put position in QWY using the April €25.00 strike option
Strategy 5: Buying 100 shares of QWY, buying the April €24.00 strike put option, and writing the April €31.00 strike call option
Strategy 6: Implementing a bear spread in QWY using the April €25.00 and April €31.00 strike options

Finally, Nuñes considers two option strategies relating to XDF.

Strategy 7: Writing both the April €75.00 strike call option and the April €75.00 strike put option on XDF
Strategy 8: Writing the February €80.00 strike call option and buying the December €80.00 strike call option on XDF

Over the past few months, Nuñes and Pereira have followed news reports on a proposed merger between XDF and one of its competitors. A government antitrust committee is currently reviewing the potential merger. Pereira expects the share price to move sharply up or down depending on whether the committee decides to approve or reject the merger next week.

Pereira asks Nuñes to recommend an option trade that might allow the firm to benefit from a significant move in the XDF share price regardless of the direction of the move.

1. Strategy 1 would require Nuñes to buy:
   A. shares of IZD.
   B. a put option on IZD.
   C. a call option on IZD.
2. Based on Exhibit 1, Nuñes should expect Strategy 2 to be *least* profitable if the share price of IZD at option expiration is:
   A. less than €91.26.
   B. between €91.26 and €95.00.
   C. more than €95.00.
3. Based on Exhibit 1, the breakeven share price of Strategy 3 is *closest* to:
   A. €92.25.
   B. €95.61.
   C. €95.82.
4. Based on Exhibit 1, the maximum loss per share that would be incurred if Strategy 4 was implemented is:
   A. €2.99.
   B. €3.99.
   C. unlimited.
5. Strategy 5 is *best* described as a:
   A. collar.
   B. straddle.
   C. bear spread.
6. Based on Exhibit 1, Strategy 5 offers:
   A. unlimited upside.
   B. a maximum profit of €2.48 per share.
   C. protection against losses if QWY's share price falls below €28.14.
7. Based on Exhibit 1, the breakeven share price for Strategy 6 is *closest* to:
   A. €22.50.
   B. €28.50.
   C. €33.50.
8. Based on Exhibit 1, the maximum gain per share that could be earned if Strategy 7 is implemented is:
   A. €5.74.
   B. €5.76.
   C. unlimited.
9. Based on Exhibit 1, the *best* explanation for Nuñes to implement Strategy 8 would be that, between the February and December expiration dates, she expects the share price of XDF to:
   A. decrease.
   B. remain unchanged.
   C. increase.
10. The option trade that Nuñes should recommend relating to the government committee's decision is a:
    A. collar.
    B. bull spread.
    C. long straddle.

CHAPTER 6

RISK MANAGEMENT

LEARNING OUTCOMES

After completing this chapter, you will be able to do the following:

- discuss features of the risk management process, risk governance, risk reduction, and an enterprise risk management system;
- evaluate strengths and weaknesses of a company's risk management process;
- describe steps in an effective enterprise risk management system;
- evaluate a company's or a portfolio's exposures to financial and nonfinancial risk factors;
- calculate and interpret value at risk (VaR) and explain its role in measuring overall and individual position market risk;
- compare the analytical (variance–covariance), historical, and Monte Carlo methods for estimating VaR and discuss the advantages and disadvantages of each;
- discuss advantages and limitations of VaR and its extensions, including cash flow at risk, earnings at risk, and tail value at risk;
- compare alternative types of stress testing and discuss advantages and disadvantages of each;
- evaluate the credit risk of an investment position, including forward contract, swap, and option positions;
- demonstrate the use of risk budgeting, position limits, and other methods for managing market risk;
- demonstrate the use of exposure limits, marking to market, collateral, netting arrangements, credit standards, and credit derivatives to manage credit risk;
- discuss the Sharpe ratio, risk-adjusted return on capital, return over maximum drawdown, and the Sortino ratio as measures of risk-adjusted performance;
- demonstrate the use of VaR and stress testing in setting capital requirements.

SUMMARY OVERVIEW

Financial markets reward competence and knowledge in risk management and punish mistakes. Portfolio managers must therefore study and understand the discipline of successful risk management. In this reading, we have introduced basic concepts and techniques of risk management and made the following points:

- Risk management is a process involving the identification of the exposures to risk, the establishment of appropriate ranges for exposures, the continuous measurement of these exposures, and the execution of appropriate adjustments to bring the actual level and desired level of risk into alignment. The process involves continuous monitoring of exposures and new policies, preferences, and information.
- Typically, risks should be minimized wherever and whenever companies lack comparative advantages in the associated markets, activities, or lines of business.
- Risk governance refers to the process of setting risk management policies and standards for an organization. Senior management, which is ultimately responsible for all organizational activities, must oversee the process.
- Enterprise risk management is a centralized risk management system whose distinguishing feature is a firm-wide or across-enterprise perspective on risk.
- Financial risk refers to all risks derived from events in the external financial markets. Nonfinancial risk refers to all other forms of risk. Financial risk includes market risk (risk related to interest rates, exchange rates, stock prices, and commodity prices), credit risk, and liquidity risk. The primary sources of nonfinancial risk are operations risk, model risk, settlement risk, regulatory risk, legal risk, tax risk, and accounting risk.
- Traditional measures of market risk include linear approximations such as beta for stocks, duration for fixed income, and delta for options, as well as second-order estimation techniques such as convexity and gamma. For products with option-like characteristics, techniques exist to measure the impact of changes in volatility (vega) and the passage of time (theta). Sensitivity to movements in the correlation among assets is also relevant for certain types of instruments.
- Value at risk (VaR) estimates the minimum loss that a party would expect to experience with a given probability over a specified period of time. Using the complementary probability (i.e., 100% minus the given probability stated as a percent), VaR can be expressed as a maximum loss at a given confidence level. VaR users must make decisions regarding appropriate time periods, confidence intervals, and specific VaR methodologies.
- The analytical or variance–covariance method can be used to determine VaR under the assumption that returns are normally distributed by subtracting a multiple of the standard deviation from the expected return, where the multiple is determined by the desired probability level. The advantage of the method is its simplicity. Its disadvantages are that returns are not normally distributed in any reliable sense and that the method does not work well when portfolios contain options and other derivatives.
- The historical method estimates VaR from data on a portfolio's performance during a historical period. The returns are ranked, and VaR is obtained by determining the return that is exceeded in a negative sense 5% or 1% (depending on the user's choice) of the time. The historical method has the advantage of being simple and not requiring the assumption of a normal distribution. Its disadvantage is that accurate historical time-series information is not always easily available, particularly for instruments such as bonds and options, which behave differently at different points in their life spans.
- Monte Carlo simulation estimates VaR by generating random returns and determining the 5% or 1% (depending on the user's choice) worst outcomes. It has the advantages that

it does not require a normal distribution and can handle complex relationships among risks.

- VaR can be difficult to estimate, can give a wide range of values, and can lead to a false sense of security that risk is accurately measured and under control. VaR for individual positions do not generally aggregate in a simple way to portfolio VaR. VaR also puts all emphasis on the negative outcomes, ignoring the positive outcomes. It can be difficult to calculate VaR for a large complex organization with many exposures. On the other hand, VaR is a simple and easy-to-understand risk measure that is widely accepted. It is also adaptable to a variety of uses, such as allocating capital.

- Incremental VaR measures the incremental effect of an asset on the VaR of a portfolio. Cash flow at risk and earnings at risk measure the risk to a company's cash flow or earnings instead of market value, as in the case of VaR. Tail value at risk is VaR plus the expected loss in excess of VaR, when such excess loss occurs. Stress testing is another important supplement to VaR.

- Credit risk has two dimensions, the probability of default and the associated recovery rate.

- Credit risk in a forward contract is assumed by the party to which the market value is positive. The market value represents the current value of the claim that one party has on the other. The actual payoff at expiration could differ, but the market value reflects the current value of that future claim.

- Credit risk in swaps is similar to credit risk in forward contracts. The market value represents the current value of the claim on the future payments. The party holding the positive market value assumes the credit risk at that time. For interest rate and equity swaps, credit risk is greatest near the middle of the life of the swap. For currency swaps with payment of notional principal, credit risk is greatest near the end of the life of the swap.

- Credit risk in options is one-sided. Because the seller is paid immediately and in full, she faces no credit risk. By contrast, the buyer faces the risk that the seller will not meet her obligations in the event of exercise. The market value of the option is the current value of the future claim the buyer has on the seller.

- VaR can be used to measure credit risk. The interpretation is the same as with standard VaR, but a credit-based VaR is more complex because it must interact with VaR based on market risk. Credit risk arises only when market risk results in gains to trading. Credit VaR must take into account the complex interaction of market movements, the possibility of default, and recovery rates. Credit VaR is also difficult to aggregate across markets and counterparties.

- Risk budgeting is the process of establishing policies to allocate the finite resource of risk capacity to business units that must assume exposure in order to generate return. Risk budgeting has also been applied to allocation of funds to investment managers.

- The various methods of controlling credit risk include setting exposure limits for individual counterparties, exchanging cash values that reflect mark-to-market levels, posting collateral, netting, setting minimum credit, using special-purpose vehicles that have higher credit ratings than the companies that own them, and using credit derivatives.

- Among the measures of risk-adjusted performance that have been used in a portfolio context are the Sharpe ratio, risk-adjusted return on capital, return over maximum drawdown, and the Sortino ratio. The Sharpe ratio uses standard deviation, measuring total risk as the risk measure. Risk-adjusted return on capital accounts for risk using capital at risk. The Sortino ratio measures risk using downside deviation, which computes volatility using only rate-of-return data points below a minimum acceptable return. Return over maximum drawdown uses maximum drawdown as a risk measure.

- Methods for allocating capital include nominal position limits, VaR-based position limits, maximum loss limits, internal capital requirements, and regulatory capital requirements.

PROBLEMS

1. Discuss the difference between centralized and decentralized risk management systems, including the advantages and disadvantages of each.

2. Stewart Gilchrist follows the automotive industry, including Ford Motor Company. Based on Ford's 2003 annual report, Gilchrist writes the following summary:

   Ford Motor Company has businesses in several countries around the world. Ford frequently has expenditures and receipts denominated in non-US currencies, including purchases and sales of finished vehicles and production parts, subsidiary dividends, investments in non-US operations, etc. Ford uses a variety of commodities in the production of motor vehicles, such as non-ferrous metals, precious metals, ferrous alloys, energy, and plastics/resins. Ford typically purchases these commodities from outside suppliers. To finance its operations, Ford uses a variety of funding sources, such as commercial paper, term debt, and lines of credit from major commercial banks. The company invests any surplus cash in securities of various types and maturities, the value of which are subject to fluctuations in interest rates. Ford has a credit division, which provides financing to customers wanting to purchase Ford's vehicles on credit. Overall, Ford faces several risks. To manage some of its risks, Ford invests in fixed-income instruments and derivative contracts. Some of these investments do not rely on a clearing house and instead effect settlement through the execution of bilateral agreements.

   Based on the above discussion, recommend and justify the risk exposures that should be reported as part of an Enterprise Risk Management System for Ford Motor Company.

3. NatWest Markets (NWM) was the investment banking arm of National Westminster Bank, one of the largest banks in the United Kingdom. On 28 February 1997, NWM revealed that a substantial loss had been uncovered in its trading books. During the 1990s, NatWest was engaged in trading interest rate options and swaptions on several underlying currencies. This trading required setting appropriate prices of the options by the traders at NatWest. A key parameter in setting the price of an interest rate option is the implied volatility of the underlying asset—that is, the interest rate on a currency. In contrast to other option parameters that affect the option prices, such as duration to maturity and exercise price, implied volatility is not directly observable and must be estimated. Many option pricing models imply that the implied volatility should be the same for all options on the same underlying, irrespective of their exercise price or maturity. In practice, however, implied volatility is often observed to have a curvilinear relationship with the option's moneyness (i.e., whether the option is out of the money, at the money, or in the money), a relationship sometimes called the *volatility smile*. Implied volatility tended to be higher for out-of-the-money options than for at-the-money options on the same underlying.

   NWM prices on certain contracts tended to consistently undercut market prices, as if the out-of-the money options were being quoted at implied volatilities that were too low. When trading losses mounted in an interest rate option contract, a trader undertook a series of off-market-price transactions between the options portfolio and a swaptions portfolio to transfer the losses to a type of contract where losses were easier to conceal.

Practice Problems and Solutions: 1–18 taken from *Managing Investment Portfolios: A Dynamic Process*, Third Edition, John L. Maginn, CFA, Donald L. Tuttle, CFA, Jerald E. Pinto, CFA, and Dennis W. McLeavey, CFA, editors. © 2007 CFA Institute. All other problems and solutions © CFA Institute. All rights reserved.

A subsequent investigation revealed that the back office did not independently value the trading positions in question and that lapses in trade reconciliation had occurred.

What type or types of risk were inadequately managed in the above case?

4. Sue Ellicott supervises the trading function at an asset management firm. In conducting an in-house risk management training session for traders, Ellicott elicits the following statements from traders:

Trader 1   "Liquidity risk is not a major concern for buyers of a security as opposed to sellers."

Trader 2   "In general, derivatives can be used to substantially reduce the liquidity risk of a security."

Ellicott and the traders then discuss two recent cases of a similar risk exposure in an identical situation that one trader (Trader A) hedged and another trader (Trader B) assumed as a speculation. A participant in the discussion makes the following statement concerning the contrasting treatment:

Trader 3   "Our traders have considerable experience and expertise in analyzing the risk, and this risk is related to our business. Trader B was justified in speculating on the risk within the limits of his risk allocation."

State and justify whether each trader's statement is correct or incorrect.

5. A large trader on the government bond desk of a major bank loses €20 million in a year, in the process reducing the desk's overall profit to €10 million. Senior management, on looking into the problem, determines that the trader repeatedly violated his position limits during the year. They also determine that the bulk of the loss took place in the last two weeks of the year, when the trader increased his position dramatically and experienced 80% of his negative performance. The bank dismisses both the trader and his desk manager. The bank has an asymmetric incentive compensation contract arrangement with its traders.

A. Discuss the performance netting risk implications of this scenario.

B. Are there any reasons why the timing of the loss is particularly significant?

C. What mistakes did senior management make? Explain how these errors can be corrected.

6. Ford Credit is the branch of Ford Motor Company that provides financing to Ford's customers. For this purpose, it obtains funding from various sources. As a result of its interest rate risk management process, including derivatives, Ford Credit's debt reprices faster than its assets. This situation means that when interest rates are rising, the interest rates paid on Ford Credit's debt will increase more rapidly than the interest rates earned on assets, thereby initially reducing Ford Credit's pretax net interest income. The reverse will be true when interest rates decline.

Ford's annual report provides a quantitative measure of the sensitivity of Ford Credit's pretax net interest income to changes in interest rates. For this purpose, it uses interest rate scenarios that assume a hypothetical, instantaneous increase or decrease in interest rates of 1 percentage point across all maturities. These scenarios are compared with a base case that assumes that interest rates remain constant at existing levels. The differences between the scenarios and the base case over a 12-month period represent an estimate of the sensitivity of Ford Credit's pretax net interest income. This sensitivity as of year-end 2003 and 2002 is as follows:

	Pretax Net Interest Income Impact Given a One Percentage Point Instantaneous *Increase* in Interest Rates (in Millions)	Pretax Net Interest Income Impact Given a One Percentage Point Instantaneous *Decrease* in Interest Rates (in Millions)
December 31, 2003	($179)	$179
December 31, 2002	($153)	$156

Source: Annual Report of Ford Motor Company, 2003.

   Describe the strengths and weaknesses of the interest rate risk analysis presented in the foregoing table.

7. A. An organization's risk management function has computed that a portfolio held in one business unit has a 1% weekly value at risk (VaR) of £4.25 million. Describe what is meant in terms of a minimum loss.

    B. The portfolio of another business unit has a 99% weekly VaR of £4.25 million (stated using a confidence limit approach). Describe what is meant in terms of a maximum loss.

8. Each of the following statements about VaR is true *except*:

    A. VaR is the loss that would be exceeded with a given probability over a specific time period.

    B. Establishing a VaR involves several decisions, such as the probability and time period over which the VaR will be measured and the technique to be used.

    C. VaR will be larger when it is measured at 5% probability than when it is measured at 1% probability.

    D. VaR will be larger when it is measured over a month than when it is measured over a day.

9. Suppose you are given the following sample probability distribution of annual returns on a portfolio with a market value of $10 million.

Return on Portfolio	Probability
Less than −50%	0.005
−50% to −40%	0.005
−40% to −30%	0.010
−30% to −20%	0.015
−20% to −10%	0.015
−10% to −5%	0.165
−5% to 0%	0.250
0% to 5%	0.250
5% to 10%	0.145
10% to 20%	0.075
20% to 30%	0.025
30% to 40%	0.020
40% to 50%	0.015
Greater than 50%	0.005
	1.000

Based on this probability distribution, determine the following:
A. 1% yearly VaR.
B. 5% yearly VaR.

10. An analyst would like to know the VaR for a portfolio consisting of two asset classes: long-term government bonds issued in the United States and long-term government bonds issued in the United Kingdom. The expected monthly return on US bonds is 0.85%, and the standard deviation is 3.20%. The expected monthly return on UK bonds, in US dollars, is 0.95%, and the standard deviation is 5.26%. The correlation between the US dollar returns of UK and US bonds is 0.35. The portfolio market value is $100 million and is equally weighted between the two asset classes. Using the analytical or variance–covariance method, compute the following:
A. 5% monthly VaR.
B. 1% monthly VaR.
C. 5% weekly VaR.
D. 1% weekly VaR.

11. You invested $25,000 in the stock of Dell Computer Corporation in early 2011. You have compiled the monthly returns on Dell's stock during the period 2006–2010, as given below.

2006	2007	2008	2009	2010
−0.0214	−0.0347	−0.1824	−0.0723	−0.1017
−0.0106	−0.0566	−0.0070	−0.1021	0.0264
0.0262	0.0158	0.0010	0.1114	0.1344
−0.1196	0.0862	−0.0648	0.2257	0.0786
−0.0313	0.0675	0.2378	−0.0043	−0.1772
−0.0362	0.0609	−0.0512	0.1867	−0.0953
−0.1137	−0.0203	0.1229	−0.0255	0.0978
0.0401	0.0100	−0.1156	0.1831	−0.1110
0.0129	−0.0230	−0.2416	−0.0360	0.1020
0.0652	0.1087	−0.2597	−0.0531	0.1099
0.1196	−0.1980	−0.0844	−0.0228	−0.0816
−0.0789	−0.0012	−0.0833	0.0170	0.0250

Using the historical method, compute the following:
A. 5% monthly VaR.
B. 1% monthly VaR.

12. Consider a $10 million portfolio of stocks. You perform a Monte Carlo simulation to estimate the VaR for this portfolio. You choose to perform this simulation using a normal distribution of returns for the portfolio, with an expected annual return of 14.8% and a

standard deviation of 20.5%. You generate 700 random outcomes of annual return for this portfolio, of which the worst 40 outcomes are given below.

−0.400	−0.320	−0.295	−0.247
−0.398	−0.316	−0.282	−0.233
−0.397	−0.314	−0.277	−0.229
−0.390	−0.310	−0.273	−0.226
−0.355	−0.303	−0.273	−0.223
−0.350	−0.301	−0.261	−0.222
−0.347	−0.301	−0.259	−0.218
−0.344	−0.300	−0.253	−0.216
−0.343	−0.298	−0.251	−0.215
−0.333	−0.296	−0.248	−0.211

Using the above information, compute the following:
A. 5% annual VaR.
B. 1% annual VaR.

13. A. A firm runs an investment portfolio consisting of stocks as well as options on stocks. Management would like to determine the VaR for this portfolio and is thinking about which technique to use. Discuss a problem with using the analytical or variance–covariance method for determining the VaR of this portfolio.

    B. Describe a situation in which an organization might logically select each of the three VaR methodologies.

14. An organization's 5% daily VaR shows a number fairly consistently around €3 million. A backtest of the calculation reveals that, as expected under the calculation, daily portfolio losses in excess of €3 million tend to occur about once a month. When such losses do occur, however, they typically are more than double the VaR estimate. The portfolio contains a very large short options position.

    A. Is the VaR calculation accurate?
    B. How can the VaR figure best be interpreted?
    C. What additional measures might the organization take to increase the accuracy of its overall exposure assessments?

15. Indicate which of the following statements about credit risk is (are) false, and explain why.

    A. Because credit losses occur often, it is easy to assess the probability of a credit loss.
    B. One element of credit risk is the possibility that the counterparty to a contract will default on an obligation to another (i.e., third) party.
    C. Like the buyer of a European-style option, the buyer of an American-style option faces no current credit risk until the expiration of the option.

16. Ricardo Colón, an analyst in the investment management division of a financial services firm, is developing an earnings forecast for a local oil services company. The company's income is closely linked to the price of oil. Furthermore, the company derives the majority of its income from sales to the United States. The economy of the company's home country depends significantly on export oil sales to the United States. As a result, movements in world oil prices in US dollar terms and the US dollar value of the home country's currency are strongly positively correlated. A decline in oil prices would reduce the company's sales in US dollar terms, all else being equal. On the other hand, the appreciation of the home

country's currency relative to the US dollar would reduce the company's sales in terms of the home currency.

According to Colón's research, Raúl Rodriguez, the company's chief risk officer, has made the following statement:

"The company has rejected hedging the market risk of a decline in oil prices by selling oil futures and hedging the currency risk of a depreciation of the US dollar relative to our home currency by buying home currency futures in US markets. We have decided that a more effective risk management strategy for our company is to not hedge either market risk or currency risk."

- A. State whether the company's decision to not hedge market risk was correct. Justify your answer with one reason.
- B. State whether the company's decision to not hedge currency risk was correct. Justify your answer with one reason.
- C. Critique the risk management strategy adopted.

17. Tony Smith believes that the price of a particular underlying, currently selling at $96, will increase substantially in the next six months, so he purchases a European call option expiring in six months on this underlying. The call option has an exercise price of $101 and sells for $6.
    - A. How much is the current credit risk, if any?
    - B. How much is the current value of the potential credit risk, if any?
    - C. Which party bears the credit risk(s), Tony Smith or the seller?

18. Following are four methods for calculating risk-adjusted performance: the Sharpe ratio, risk-adjusted return on capital (RAROC), return over maximum drawdown (RoMAD), and the Sortino ratio. Compare and contrast the measure of risk that each method uses.

The following information relates to Questions 19–24

Monika Kreuzer chairs the risk management committee for DGI Investors, a European money management firm. The agenda for the 1 June committee meeting includes three issues concerning client portfolios:

1. Estimating a new value at risk (VaR) for the Stimson Industries portfolio.
2. Answering questions from Kalton Corporation managers.
3. Revising the VaR for Muth Company given new capital market expectations.

1. VaR for Stimson Industries. DGI currently provides a 5% yearly VaR on the equity portfolio that it manages for Stimson. The €50 million portfolio has an expected annual return of 9.6% and an annual standard deviation of 18.0%. With a standard normal distribution, 5% of the possible outcomes are 1.65 standard deviations or more below the mean. Using the analytical (variance–covariance) method for calculating VaR, DGI estimates the 5% yearly VaR to be €10.05 million. Assuming that monthly returns are independent, committee member Eric Stulz wants to estimate a 5% *monthly* VaR for Stimson's portfolio.

Stulz asks his fellow committee members for feedback on the following statements about VaR in a report he is preparing for Stimson Industries:

Statement #1:   "Establishing a VaR involves several decisions, such as the probability and time period over which the VaR will be measured and the technique to be used."

Statement #2:   "A portfolio's VaR will be larger when it is measured at a 5% proba-
                bility than when it is measured at a 1% probability."

Statement #3:   "A portfolio's VaR will be larger when it is measured over a month
                than when it is measured over a day."

2. Questions from Kalton Corporation Managers. Kalton Corporation has two large derivatives positions with a London securities house. The first position is a long forward currency contract to buy pounds at €1.4500. The current exchange rate is €1.4000 per pound. The second
position is a long put position on the DJ Euro STOXX Index with a strike price of 305.00. The
current closing price of the index is 295.00. A Kalton manager has written, "I am concerned
about the risks of these two large positions. Who is bearing the credit risks, Kalton Corporation
or the counterparty (the London securities house)?" Kreuzer suggests that DGI reply: "Kalton
Corporation is bearing the credit risk of the currency forward contract, but the London securities house is bearing the credit risk of the put option on the DJ Euro STOXX Index."

Because they believe that the credit risk in corporate bonds is going to decline, Kalton
Corporation managers have decided to increase Kalton's credit risk exposure in corporate
bonds. They have asked Kreuzer and the risk management committee to recommend derivatives positions to accomplish this change.

3. Revising the VaR for Muth Company. Kreuzer provides a variety of statistics to Muth,
for whom DGI manages a portfolio composed of 50% in Asia-Pacific equities and 50% in
European equities. One of the statistics that Kreuzer supplies Muth is a 5% monthly VaR estimate based on the analytical (variance–covariance) method. Kreuzer is concerned that changes
in the market outlook will affect Muth's risk. DGI is updating its capital market expectations,
which will include 1) an increase in the expected return on Asia-Pacific equities and 2) an
increase in the correlation between Asia-Pacific equities and European equities. Kreuzer comments: "Considered independently, and assuming that other variables are held constant, each
of these changes in capital market expectations will increase the monthly VaR estimate for the
Muth portfolio."

Kreuzer also discusses the limitations and strengths of applying VaR to the Muth portfolio. She states that: "One of the advantages of VaR is that the VaR of individual positions
can be simply aggregated to find the portfolio VaR." Kreuzer also describes how VaR can be
supplemented with performance evaluation measures, such as the Sharpe ratio. She states: "The
Sharpe ratio is widely used for calculating a risk-adjusted return, although it can be an inaccurate measure when applied to portfolios with significant options positions."

19. The monthly VaR that Stulz wants to estimate for the Stimson portfolio is *closest* to:
    A. €0.8 million.
    B. €2.9 million.
    C. €3.9 million.
20. Regarding the three statements in the report that Stulz is preparing for Stimson Industries,
    the statement that is *incorrect* is:
    A. Statement #1.
    B. Statement #2.
    C. Statement #3.
21. Regarding Kalton's two derivatives positions, is Kreuzer correct about which party is bear-
    ing the credit risk of the currency forward contract and the put option on the DJ Euro
    STOXX Index, respectively?

	Currency Forward Contract	Put Option on the DJ Euro STOXX Index
A.	No	No
B.	No	Yes
C.	Yes	Yes

22. To make the desired change in Kalton's credit risk exposure in corporate bonds, Kreuzer could recommend that Kalton take a position as a:
    A. seller in a credit default swap.
    B. buyer in a credit default swap.
    C. buyer of a put option on a corporate bond.

23. Is Kreuzer correct in predicting the independent effects of the increase in the expected return and the increase in the correlation, respectively, on the calculated VaR of the Muth portfolio?

	Effect of Increase in the Expected Return	Effect of Increase in the Correlation
A.	No	No
B.	No	Yes
C.	Yes	No

24. Are Kreuzer's statements about an advantage of VaR and about the Sharpe ratio, respectively, correct?

	Statement about an Advantage of VaR	Statement about the Sharpe Ratio
A.	No	No
B.	No	Yes
C.	Yes	Yes

CHAPTER 7

RISK MANAGEMENT APPLICATIONS OF FORWARD AND FUTURES STRATEGIES

LEARNING OUTCOMES

After completing this chapter, you will be able to do the following:

- demonstrate the use of equity futures contracts to achieve a target beta for a stock portfolio and calculate and interpret the number of futures contracts required;
- construct a synthetic stock index fund using cash and stock index futures (equitizing cash);
- explain the use of stock index futures to convert a long stock position into synthetic cash;
- demonstrate the use of equity and bond futures to adjust the allocation of a portfolio between equity and debt;
- demonstrate the use of futures to adjust the allocation of a portfolio across equity sectors and to gain exposure to an asset class in advance of actually committing funds to the asset class;
- explain exchange rate risk and demonstrate the use of forward contracts to reduce the risk associated with a future receipt or payment in a foreign currency;
- explain the limitations to hedging the exchange rate risk of a foreign market portfolio and discuss feasible strategies for managing such risk.

SUMMARY OVERVIEW

- A borrower can lock in the rate that will be set at a future date on a single-payment loan by entering into a long position in an FRA. The FRA obligates the borrower to make a fixed interest payment and receive a floating interest payment, thereby protecting the borrower if the loan rate is higher than the fixed rate in the FRA but also eliminating gains if the loan rate is lower than the fixed rate in the FRA.

- The duration of a bond futures contract is determined as the duration of the bond underlying the futures contract as of the futures expiration, based on the yield of the bond underlying the futures contract. The modified duration is obtained by dividing the duration by 1 plus the yield. The duration of a futures contract is implied by these factors and is called the implied (modified) duration.
- The implied yield of a futures contract is the yield implied by the futures price on the bond underlying the futures contract as of the futures expiration.
- The yield beta is the sensitivity of the yield on a bond portfolio relative to the implied yield on the futures contract.
- The number of bond futures contracts required to change the duration of a bond portfolio is based on the ratio of the market value of the bonds to the futures price multiplied by the difference between the target or desired modified duration and the actual modified duration, divided by the implied modified duration of the futures.
- The actual adjusted duration of a bond portfolio may not equal the desired duration for a number of reasons, including that the yield beta may be inaccurate or unstable or the bonds could contain call features or default risk. In addition, duration is a measure of instantaneous risk and may not accurately capture the risk over a long horizon without frequent portfolio adjustments.
- The number of equity futures contracts required to change the beta of an equity portfolio is based on the ratio of the market value of the stock to the futures price times the difference between the target or desired beta and the actual beta, divided by the beta of the futures.
- A long position in stock is equivalent to a long position in futures and a long position in a risk-free bond; therefore, it is possible to synthetically create a long position in stock by buying futures on stock and a risk-free bond. This process is called equitizing cash and can be used to create a synthetic stock index fund.
- A long position in cash is equivalent to a long position in stock and a short position in stock futures. Therefore, it is possible to synthetically create a long position in cash by buying stock and selling futures.
- The allocation of a portfolio between equity and debt can be adjusted using stock index and bond futures. Buy futures to increase the allocation to an asset class, and sell futures to decrease the allocation to an asset class.
- The allocation of a bond portfolio between cash and high-duration bonds can be adjusted by using bond futures. Sell futures to increase the allocation to cash, and buy futures to increase the allocation to long-term bonds.
- The allocation of an equity portfolio among different equity sectors can be adjusted by using stock index futures. Sell futures on an index representing one sector to decrease the allocation to that sector, and buy futures on an index representing another sector to increase the allocation to that sector.
- A portfolio manager can buy bond or stock index futures to take a position in an asset class without having cash to actually invest in the asset class. This type of strategy is sometimes used in anticipation of the receipt of a sum of cash at a later date, which will then be invested in the asset class and the futures position will be closed.
- Transaction exposure is the risk associated with a foreign exchange rate on a specific business transaction such as a purchase or sale. Translation exposure is the risk associated with the conversion of foreign financial statements into domestic currency. Economic exposure is the risk associated with changes in the relative attractiveness of products and services offered for sale, arising out of the competitive effects of changes in exchange rates.

- The risk of a future foreign currency receipt can be eliminated by selling a forward contract on the currency. This transaction locks in the rate at which the foreign currency will be converted to the domestic currency.
- The risk of a future foreign currency payment can be eliminated by buying a forward contract on the currency. This transaction locks in the rate at which the domestic currency will be converted to the foreign currency.
- It is not possible to invest in a foreign equity market and precisely hedge the currency risk only. To hedge the currency risk, one must know the exact amount of foreign currency that will be available at a future date. Without locking in the equity return, it is not possible to know how much foreign currency will be available.
- It is possible to hedge the foreign equity market return and accept the exchange rate risk or hedge the foreign equity market return *and* hedge the exchange rate risk. By hedging the equity market return, one would know the proper amount of currency that would be available at a later date and could use a futures or forward contract to hedge the currency risk. The equity return, however, would equal the risk-free rate.
- Forward contracts are usually preferred over futures contracts when the risk is related to an event on a specific date, such as an interest rate reset. Forward contracts on foreign currency are usually preferred over futures contracts, primarily because of the liquidity of the market. Futures contracts require margins and daily settlements but are guaranteed against credit losses and may be preferred when credit concerns are an issue. Either contract may be preferred or required if there are restrictions on the use of the other. Dealers use both instruments in managing their risk, occasionally preferring one instrument and sometimes preferring the other. Forward contracts are preferred if privacy is important.
- Futures and forwards, as well as virtually all derivatives, have an advantage over transactions in the actual instruments by virtue of their significantly lower transaction costs. They also allow a portfolio manager to make changes in the risk of certain asset classes or the allocation among asset classes without disturbing the asset class or classes themselves. This feature allows the asset class managers to concentrate on their respective asset classes without being concerned about buying and selling to execute risk-altering changes or asset allocation changes.
- Although futures and forwards tend to be more liquid than their underlying assets, they are not always highly liquid. Therefore, it cannot always be assumed that futures and forwards can solve liquidity problems.

PROBLEMS

1. An investment management firm wishes to increase the beta for one of its portfolios under management from 0.95 to 1.20 for a three-month period. The portfolio has a market value of $175,000,000. The investment firm plans to use a futures contract priced at $105,790 in order to adjust the portfolio beta. The futures contract has a beta of 0.98.
   A. Calculate the number of futures contracts that should be bought or sold to achieve an increase in the portfolio beta.

Practice Problems and Solutions: *Analysis of Derivatives for the Chartered Financial Analyst® Program*, by Don M. Chance, CFA. © 2003 CFA Institute. All rights reserved.

B. At the end of three months, the overall equity market is up 5.5%. The stock portfolio under management is up 5.1%. The futures contract is priced at $111,500. Calculate the value of the overall position and the effective beta of the portfolio.

2. Consider an asset manager who wishes to create a fund with exposure to the Russell 2000 stock index. The initial amount to be invested is $300,000,000. The fund will be constructed using the Russell 2000 Index futures contract, priced at 498.30 with a $500 multiplier. The contract expires in three months. The underlying index has a dividend yield of 0.75%, and the risk-free rate is 2.35% per year.

A. Indicate how the money manager would go about constructing this synthetic index using futures.

B. Assume that at expiration, the Russell 2000 is at 594.65. Show how the synthetic position produces the same result as investment in the actual stock index.

3. An investment management firm has a client who would like to temporarily reduce his exposure to equities by converting a $25 million equity position to cash for a period of four months. The client would like this reduction to take place without liquidating his equity position. The investment management firm plans to create a synthetic cash position using an equity futures contract. This futures contract is priced at 1170.10, has a multiplier of $250, and expires in four months. The dividend yield on the underlying index is 1.25%, and the risk-free rate is 2.75%.

A. Calculate the number of futures contracts required to create synthetic cash.

B. Determine the effective amount of money committed to this risk-free transaction and the effective number of units of the stock index that are converted to cash.

C. Assume that the stock index is at 1031 when the futures contract expires. Show how this strategy is equivalent to investing the risk-free asset, cash.

4. Consider a portfolio with a 65% allocation to stocks and 35% to bonds. The portfolio has a market value of $200 million. The beta of the stock position is 1.15, and the modified duration of the bond position is 6.75. The portfolio manager wishes to increase the stock allocation to 85% and reduce the bond allocation to 15% for a period of six months. In addition to altering asset allocations, the manager would also like to increase the beta on the stock position to 1.20 and increase the modified duration of the bonds to 8.25. A stock index futures contract that expires in six months is priced at $157,500 and has a beta of 0.95. A bond futures contract that expires in six months is priced at $109,000 and has an implied modified duration of 5.25. The stock futures contract has a multiplier of one.

A. Show how the portfolio manager can achieve his goals by using stock index and bond futures. Indicate the number of contracts and whether the manager should go long or short.

B. After six months, the stock portfolio is up 5% and bonds are up 1.35%. The stock futures price is $164,005 and the bond futures price is $110,145. Compare the market value of the portfolio in which the allocation is adjusted using futures to the market value of the portfolio in which the allocation is adjusted by directly trading stocks and bonds.

5. A pension fund manager expects to receive a cash inflow of $50,000,000 in three months and wants to use futures contracts to take a $17,500,000 synthetic position in stocks and $32,500,000 in bonds today. The stock would have a beta of 1.15 and the bonds a modified duration of 7.65. A stock index futures contract with a beta of 0.93 is priced at $175,210. A bond futures contract with a modified duration of 5.65 is priced at $95,750.

A. Calculate the number of stock and bond futures contracts the fund manager would have to trade in order to synthetically take the desired position in stocks and bonds today. Indicate whether the futures positions are long or short.

    B. When the futures contracts expire in three months, stocks have declined by 5.4% and bonds have declined by 3.06%. Stock index futures are priced at $167,559, and bond futures are priced at $93,586. Show that profits on the futures positions are essentially the same as the change in the value of stocks and bonds during the three-month period.

6. A. Consider a US company, GateCorp, that exports products to the United Kingdom. GateCorp has just closed a sale worth £200,000,000. The amount will be received in two months. Because it will be paid in pounds, the US company bears the exchange risk. In order to hedge this risk, GateCorp intends to use a forward contract that is priced at $1.4272 per pound. Indicate how the company would go about constructing the hedge. Explain what happens when the forward contract expires in two months.

    B. ABCorp is a US-based company that frequently imports raw materials from Australia. It has just entered into a contract to purchase A$175,000,000 worth of raw wool, to be paid in one month. ABCorp fears that the Australian dollar will strengthen, thereby raising the US dollar cost. A forward contract is available and is priced at $0.5249 per Australian dollar. Indicate how ABCorp would go about constructing a hedge. Explain what happens when the forward contract expires in one month.

CHAPTER 8

RISK MANAGEMENT APPLICATIONS OF OPTION STRATEGIES

LEARNING OUTCOMES

After completing this chapter, you will be able to do the following:

- compare the use of covered calls and protective puts to manage risk exposure to individual securities;
- calculate and interpret the value at expiration, profit, maximum profit, maximum loss, breakeven underlying price at expiration, and general shape of the graph for the following option strategies: bull spread, bear spread, butterfly spread, collar, straddle, box spread;
- calculate the effective annual rate for a given interest rate outcome when a borrower (lender) manages the risk of an anticipated loan using an interest rate call (put) option;
- calculate the payoffs for a series of interest rate outcomes when a floating rate loan is combined with 1) an interest rate cap, 2) an interest rate floor, or 3) an interest rate collar;
- explain why and how a dealer delta hedges an option position, why delta changes, and how the dealer adjusts to maintain the delta hedge;
- interpret the gamma of a delta-hedged portfolio and explain how gamma changes as in-the-money and out-of-the-money options move toward expiration.

SUMMARY OVERVIEW

- The profit from buying a call is the value at expiration, $\max(0, S_T - X)$, minus c_0, the option premium. The maximum profit is infinite, and the maximum loss is the option premium. The breakeven underlying price at expiration is the exercise price plus the option premium. When one sells a call, these results are reversed.

- The profit from buying a put is the value at expiration, $\max(0, X - S_T)$, minus p_0, the option premium. The maximum profit is the exercise price minus the option premium, and the maximum loss is the option premium. The breakeven underlying price at expiration is the exercise price minus the option premium. When one sells a put, these results are reversed.
- The profit from a covered call—the purchase of the underlying and sale of a call—is the value at expiration, $S_T - \max(0, S_T - X)$, minus $(S_0 - c_0)$, the cost of the underlying minus the option premium. The maximum profit is the exercise price minus the original underlying price plus the option premium, and the maximum loss is the cost of the underlying less the option premium. The breakeven underlying price at expiration is the original price of the underlying minus the option premium.
- The profit from a protective put—the purchase of the underlying and a put—is the value at expiration, $S_T + \max(0, X - S_T)$, minus the cost of the underlying plus the option premium, $(S_0 + p_0)$. The maximum profit is infinite, and the maximum loss is the cost of the underlying plus the option premium minus the exercise price. The breakeven underlying price at expiration is the original price of the underlying plus the option premium.
- The profit from a bull spread—the purchase of a call at one exercise price and the sale of a call with the same expiration but a higher exercise price—is the value at expiration, $\max(0, S_T - X_1) - \max(0, S_T - X_2)$, minus the net premium, $c_1 - c_2$, which is the premium of the long option minus the premium of the short option. The maximum profit is $X_2 - X_1$ minus the net premium, and the maximum loss is the net premium. The breakeven underlying price at expiration is the lower exercise price plus the net premium.
- The profit from a bear spread—the purchase of a put at one exercise price and the sale of a put with the same expiration but a lower exercise price—is the value at expiration, $\max(0, X_2 - S_T) - \max(0, X_1 - S_T)$, minus the net premium, $p_2 - p_1$, which is the premium of the long option minus the premium of the short option. The maximum profit is $X_2 - X_1$ minus the net premium, and the maximum loss is the net premium. The breakeven underlying price at expiration is the higher exercise price minus the net premium.
- The profit from a butterfly spread—the purchase of a call at one exercise price, X_1, sale of two calls at a higher exercise price, X_2, and the purchase of a call at a higher exercise price, X_3—is the value at expiration, $\max(0, S_T - X_1) - 2\max(0, S_T - X_2), + \max(0, S_T - X_3)$, minus the net premium, $c_1 - 2c_2 + c_3$. The maximum profit is $X_2 - X_1$ minus the net premium, and the maximum loss is the net premium. The breakeven underlying prices at expiration are $2X_2 - X_1$ minus the net premium and X_1 plus the net premium. A butterfly spread can also be constructed by trading the corresponding put options.
- The profit from a collar—the holding of the underlying, the purchase of a put at one exercise price, X_1, and the sale of a call with the same expiration and a higher exercise price, X_2, and in which the premium on the put equals the premium on the call—is the value at expiration, $S_T + \max(0, X_1 - S_T) - \max(0, S_T - X_2)$, minus S_0, the original price of the underlying. The maximum profit is $X_2 - S_0$, and the maximum loss is $S_0 - X_1$. The breakeven underlying price at expiration is the initial price of the underlying.
- The profit from a straddle—a long position in a call and a put with the same exercise price and expiration—is the value at expiration, $\max(0, S_T - X) + \max(0, X - S_T)$, minus the premiums on the call and put, $c_0 + p_0$. The maximum profit is infinite, and the maximum loss is the sum of the premiums on the call and put, $c_0 + p_0$. The breakeven prices at expiration are the exercise price plus and minus the premiums on the call and put.
- A box spread is a combination of a bull spread using calls and a bear spread using puts, with one call and put at an exercise price of X_1 and another call and put at an exercise price of X_2.

The profit is the value at expiration, $X_2 - X_1$, minus the net premiums, $c_1 - c_2 + p_2 - p_1$. The transaction is risk free, and the net premium paid should be the present value of this risk-free payoff.

- A long position in an interest rate call can be used to place a ceiling on the rate on an anticipated loan from the perspective of the borrower. The call provides a payoff if the interest rate at expiration exceeds the exercise rate, thereby compensating the borrower when the rate is higher than the exercise rate. The effective interest paid on the loan is the actual interest paid minus the call payoff. The call premium must be taken into account by compounding it to the date on which the loan is taken out and deducting it from the initial proceeds received from the loan.

- A long position in an interest rate put can be used to lock in the rate on an anticipated loan from the perspective of the lender. The put provides a payoff if the interest rate at expiration is less than the exercise rate, thereby compensating the lender when the rate is lower than the exercise rate. The effective interest paid on the loan is the actual interest received plus the put payoff. The put premium must be taken into account by compounding it to the date on which the loan is taken out and adding it to initial proceeds paid out on the loan.

- An interest rate cap can be used to place an upper limit on the interest paid on a floating-rate loan from the perspective of the borrower. A cap is a series of interest rate calls, each of which is referred to as a caplet. Each caplet provides a payoff if the interest rate on the loan reset date exceeds the exercise rate, thereby compensating the borrower when the rate is higher than the exercise rate. The effective interest paid is the actual interest paid minus the caplet payoff. The premium is paid at the start and is the sum of the premiums on the component caplets.

- An interest rate floor can be used to place a lower limit on the interest received on a floating-rate loan from the perspective of the lender. A floor is a series of interest rate puts, each of which is called a floorlet. Each floorlet provides a payoff if the interest rate at the loan reset date is less than the exercise rate, thereby compensating the lender when the rate is lower than the exercise rate. The effective interest received is the actual interest plus the floorlet payoff. The premium is paid at the start and is the sum of the premiums on the component floorlets.

- An interest rate collar, which consists of a long interest rate cap at one exercise rate and a short interest rate floor at a lower exercise rate, can be used to place an upper limit on the interest paid on a floating-rate loan. The floor, however, places a lower limit on the interest paid on the floating-rate loan. Typically the floor exercise rate is set such that the premium on the floor equals the premium on the cap, so that no cash outlay is required to initiate the transaction. The effective interest is the actual interest paid minus any payoff from the long caplet plus any payoff from the short floorlet.

- Dealers offer to take positions in options and typically hedge their positions by establishing delta-neutral combinations of options and the underlying or other options. These positions require that the sensitivity of the option position with respect to the underlying be offset by a quantity of the underlying or another option. The delta will change, moving toward 1.0 for in-the-money calls (−1.0 for puts) and 0.0 for out-of-the-money options as expiration approaches. Any change in the underlying price will also change the delta. These changes in the delta necessitate buying and selling options or the underlying to maintain the delta-hedged position. Any additional funds required to buy the underlying or other options are obtained by issuing risk-free bonds. Any additional funds released from selling the underlying or other options are invested in risk-free bonds.

- The delta of an option changes as the underlying changes and as time elapses. The delta will change more rapidly with large movements in the underlying and when the option is approximately at-the-money and near expiration. These large changes in the delta will prevent a delta-hedged position from being truly risk free. Dealers usually monitor their gammas and in some cases hedge their gammas by adding other options to their positions such that the gammas offset.
- The sensitivity of an option to volatility is called the vega. An option's volatility can change, resulting in a potentially large change in the value of the option. Dealers monitor and sometimes hedge their vegas so that this risk does not impact a delta-hedged portfolio.

PROBLEMS

1. You are bullish about an underlying that is currently trading at a price of $80. You choose to go long one call option on the underlying with an exercise price of $75 and selling at $10, and go short one call option on the underlying with an exercise price of $85 and selling at $2. Both the calls expire in three months.
   A. What is the term commonly used for the position that you have taken?
   B. Determine the value at expiration and the profit for your strategy under the following outcomes:
      i. The price of the underlying at expiration is $89.
      ii. The price of the underlying at expiration is $78.
      iii. The price of the underlying at expiration is $70.
   C. Determine the following:
      i. the maximum profit.
      ii. the maximum loss.
   D. Determine the breakeven underlying price at expiration of the call options.
   E. Verify that your answer to Part D above is correct.
2. You expect a currency to depreciate with respect to the US dollar. The currency is currently trading at a price of $0.75. You decide to go long one put option on the currency with an exercise price of $0.85 and selling at $0.15, and go short one put option on the currency with an exercise price of $0.70 and selling at $0.03. Both the puts expire in three months.
   A. What is the term commonly used for the position that you have taken?
   B. Determine the value at expiration and the profit for your strategy under the following outcomes:
      i. The price of the currency at expiration is $0.87.
      ii. The price of the currency at expiration is $0.78.
      iii. The price of the currency at expiration is $0.68.
   C. Determine the following:
      i. the maximum profit.
      ii. the maximum loss.
   D. Determine the breakeven underlying price at the expiration of the put options.
   E. Verify that your answer to Part D above is correct.

Practice Problems and Solutions: *Analysis of Derivatives for the Chartered Financial Analyst® Program*, by Don M. Chance, CFA. © 2003 CFA Institute. All rights reserved.

3. A stock is currently trading at a price of $114. You construct a butterfly spread using calls of three different strike prices on this stock, with the calls expiring at the same time. You go long one call with an exercise price of $110 and selling at $8, go short two calls with an exercise price of $115 and selling at $5, and go long one call with an exercise price of $120 and selling at $3.
   A. Determine the value at expiration and the profit for your strategy under the following outcomes:
      i. The price of the stock at the expiration of the calls is $106.
      ii. The price of the stock at the expiration of the calls is $110.
      iii. The price of the stock at the expiration of the calls is $115.
      iv. The price of the stock at the expiration of the calls is $120.
      v. The price of the stock at the expiration of the calls is $123.
   B. Determine the following:
      i. the maximum profit.
      ii. the maximum loss.
      iii. the stock price at which you would realize the maximum profit.
      iv. the stock price at which you would incur the maximum loss.
   C. Determine the breakeven underlying price at expiration of the call options.
4. A stock is currently trading at a price of $114. You construct a butterfly spread using puts of three different strike prices on this stock, with the puts expiring at the same time. You go long one put with an exercise price of $110 and selling at $3.50, go short two puts with an exercise price of $115 and selling at $6, and go long one put with an exercise price of $120 and selling at $9.
   A. Determine the value at expiration and the profit for your strategy under the following outcomes:
      i. The price of the stock at the expiration of the puts is $106.
      ii. The price of the stock at the expiration of the puts is $110.
      iii. The price of the stock at the expiration of the puts is $115.
      iv. The price of the stock at the expiration of the puts is $120.
      v. The price of the stock at the expiration of the puts is $123.
   B. Determine the following:
      i. the maximum profit.
      ii. the maximum loss.
      iii. the stock price at which you would realize the maximum profit.
      iv. the stock price at which you would incur the maximum loss.
   C. Determine the breakeven underlying price at expiration of the put options.
   D. Verify that your answer to Part C above is correct.
5. A stock is currently trading at a price of $80. You decide to place a collar on this stock. You purchase a put option on the stock, with an exercise price of $75 and a premium of $3.50. You simultaneously sell a call option on the stock with the same maturity and the same premium as the put option. This call option has an exercise price of $90.
   A. Determine the value at expiration and the profit for your strategy under the following outcomes:
      i. The price of the stock at expiration of the options is $92.
      ii. The price of the stock at expiration of the options is $90.
      iii. The price of the stock at expiration of the options is $82.
      iv. The price of the stock at expiration of the options is $75.
      v. The price of the stock at expiration of the options is $70.

B. Determine the following:
    i. the maximum profit.
    ii. the maximum loss.
    iii. the stock price at which you would realize the maximum profit.
    iv. the stock price at which you would incur the maximum loss.
C. Determine the breakeven underlying price at expiration of the put options.

6. You believe that the market will be volatile in the near future, but you do not feel particularly strongly about the direction of the movement. With this expectation, you decide to buy both a call and a put with the same exercise price and the same expiration on the same underlying stock trading at $28. You buy one call option and one put option on this stock, both with an exercise price of $25. The premium on the call is $4 and the premium on the put is $1.

A. What is the term commonly used for the position that you have taken?
B. Determine the value at expiration and the profit for your strategy under the following outcomes:
    i. The price of the stock at expiration is $35.
    ii. The price of the stock at expiration is $29.
    iii. The price of the stock at expiration is $25.
    iv. The price of the stock at expiration is $20.
    v. The price of the stock at expiration is $15.
C. Determine the following:
    i. the maximum profit.
    ii. the maximum loss.
D. Determine the breakeven stock price at expiration of the options.

The following information relates to Questions 7–12

Stanley Singh, CFA, is the risk manager at SS Asset Management. Singh works with individual clients to manage their investment portfolios. One client, Sherman Hopewell, is worried about how short-term market fluctuations over the next three months might impact his equity position in Walnut Corporation. While Hopewell is concerned about short-term downside price movements, he wants to remain invested in Walnut shares as he remains positive about its long-term performance. Hopewell has asked Singh to recommend an option strategy that will keep him invested in Walnut shares while protecting against a short-term price decline. Singh gathers the information in Exhibit 1 to explore various strategies to address Hopewell's concerns.

EXHIBIT 1   Walnut Corporation Current Stock Price: $67.79 Walnut Corporation European Options

Exercise Price	Market Call Price	Call Delta	Market Put Price	Put Delta
$ 55.00	$ 12.83	4.7	$ 0.24	−16.7
$ 65.00	$ 3.65	12.0	$ 1.34	−16.9
$ 67.50	$ 1.99	16.5	$ 2.26	−15.3
$ 70.00	$ 0.91	22.2	$ 3.70	−12.9
$ 80.00	$ 0.03	35.8	$ 12.95	−5.0

Note: Each option has 106 days remaining until expiration.

Another client, Nigel French, is a trader who does not currently own shares of Walnut Corporation. French has told Singh that he believes that Walnut shares will experience a large move in price after the upcoming quarterly earnings release in two weeks. However, French tells Singh he is unsure which direction the stock will move. French asks Singh to recommend an option strategy that would allow him to profit should the share price move in either direction.

A third client, Wanda Tills, does not currently own Walnut shares and has asked Singh to explain the profit potential of three strategies using options in Walnut: a bull call spread, a straddle, and a butterfly spread. In addition, Tills asks Singh to explain the gamma of a call option. In response, Singh prepares a memo to be shared with Tills that provides a discussion of gamma and presents his analysis on three option strategies:

Strategy 1: A straddle position at the $67.50 strike option
Strategy 2: A bull call spread using the $65 and $70 strike options
Strategy 3: A butterfly spread using the $65, $67.50, and $70 strike call options

7. The option strategy Singh is *most likely* to recommend to Hopewell is a:
   A. collar.
   B. covered call.
   C. protective put.

8. The option strategy that Singh is *most likely* to recommend to French is a:
   A. straddle.
   B. butterfly.
   C. box spread.

9. Based upon Exhibit 1, Strategy 1 is profitable when the share price at expiration is *closest* to:
   A. $63.24.
   B. $65.24.
   C. $69.49.

10. Based upon Exhibit 1, the maximum profit, on a per share basis, from investing in Strategy 2, is *closest* to:
    A. $2.26.
    B. $2.74.
    C. $5.00.

11. Based upon Exhibit 1, and assuming the market price of Walnut's shares at expiration is $66, the profit or loss, on a per share basis, from investing in Strategy 3, is *closest* to:
    A. −$1.57.
    B. $0.42.
    C. $1.00.

12. Based on the data in Exhibit 1, Singh would advise Tills that the call option with the *largest* gamma would have a strike price *closest* to:
    A. $ 55.
    B. $ 67.50.
    C. $ 80.

CHAPTER 9

RISK MANAGEMENT APPLICATIONS OF SWAP STRATEGIES

LEARNING OUTCOMES

After completing this chapter, you will be able to do the following:

- demonstrate how an interest rate swap can be used to convert a floating-rate (fixed-rate) loan to a fixed-rate (floating-rate) loan;
- calculate and interpret the duration of an interest rate swap;
- explain the effect of an interest rate swap on an entity's cash flow risk;
- determine the notional principal value needed on an interest rate swap to achieve a desired level of duration in a fixed-income portfolio;
- explain how a company can generate savings by issuing a loan or bond in its own currency and using a currency swap to convert the obligation into another currency;
- demonstrate how a firm can use a currency swap to convert a series of foreign cash receipts into domestic cash receipts;
- explain how equity swaps can be used to diversify a concentrated equity portfolio, provide international diversification to a domestic portfolio, and alter portfolio allocations to stocks and bonds;
- demonstrate the use of an interest rate swaption (1) to change the payment pattern of an anticipated future loan and (2) to terminate a swap.

SUMMARY OVERVIEW

- A floating-rate loan can be converted to a fixed-rate loan by entering into an interest rate swap to pay a fixed rate and receive a floating rate. The floating cash flows offset, leaving the borrower with a net fixed payment. Likewise, a fixed-rate loan can be converted to a floating-rate loan by entering into an interest rate swap to pay a floating rate and receive a fixed rate. The fixed cash flows offset, leaving the party paying a floating rate.

- To obtain the duration of an interest rate swap, consider the difference between the duration of a fixed-rate bond and the duration of a floating-rate bond. The latter is close to zero, leaving the duration of an interest rate swap close to that of a fixed-rate bond. If the party pays a fixed rate and receives a floating rate, the duration of the position is that of the equivalent floating-rate bond minus that of the equivalent fixed-rate bond.
- When a floating-rate loan is converted to a fixed-rate loan, the resulting duration is that of a fixed-rate loan. The duration of a fixed-rate loan is normally much higher than that of a floating-rate loan, which has a duration relatively close to zero. Compared with a floating-rate loan, however, a fixed-rate loan has stable cash flows, which reduce cash flow risk, but has a much greater duration, which increases market value risk.
- The notional principal on an interest rate swap added to a position to adjust its overall duration is determined by the existing duration of the portfolio, the duration of the swap, the desired duration, and the market value of the portfolio. A swap can be used to change the duration of the position without changing the market value.
- An interest rate swap can be used to manage the risk related to a structured note with a coupon at a multiple of a floating rate by adjusting the notional principal on the swap to reflect the coupon multiple for the structured note. The swap should be a receive-floating, pay-fixed swap.
- An interest rate swap can be used to manage the risk of the issuance of an inverse floating-rate note by paying the floating rate to the swap dealer. When interest rates rise (fall), the inverse floater payments decrease (increase), and this effect is passed on to the dealer, which in turn pays a fixed rate.
- A loan in one currency can be converted into a loan in another currency by entering into a currency swap in which it pays interest in one currency and receives interest in the currency in which it makes its loan interest payments. This strategy leaves the borrower paying interest in a different currency than the one in which the loan interest is paid. To offset the principal payment, the currency swap should provide for payment of the notional principal as well.
- Converting a loan in one currency into a loan in another using a currency swap can offer savings because a borrower can normally issue debt at a more attractive rate in its own currency. By entering into a swap with a dealer that can operate more efficiently in global markets, the borrower can effectively convert its domestic debt into foreign debt. In addition, by engaging in the currency swap rather than borrowing in the desired currency in the first place, the borrower takes on a small amount of credit risk that can generate savings if no default takes place.
- The party to a currency swap would make the payments be fixed or floating depending on whether a loan paired with the currency swap is made at a fixed or floating rate and whether the party wants to make payments at a fixed or floating rate. This decision is usually made based on the expected direction of interest rates.
- A series of foreign cash receipts can be combined with a currency swap with no notional principal payments to convert the receipts into domestic currency cash flows. The foreign interest payments on the currency swap must equal the amounts of the foreign cash flows.
- In a dual-currency bond, the interest is paid in one currency and the principal is paid in another. A borrower issuing a dual-currency bond can use the proceeds to buy a bond denominated in the currency of the principal repayment on the dual-currency bond. It can then enter into a currency swap with no notional principal payment, enabling it to fund the

interest payments from the dual-currency bond in one currency and make interest payments in another currency.

- An equity swap can be used to provide diversification to a concentrated portfolio by having the party pay the return on the stock that makes up too large a portion of the portfolio and receive the return on a diversified market proxy.

- An equity swap can add international diversification to a domestic portfolio by having the party pay the return on a domestic market benchmark and receive the return on an international market benchmark.

- An equity swap can be used to change the allocation between stock and bond asset classes by having the party pay the return on the asset class in which it wants to reduce its exposure and receive the return on the asset class in which it wants to increase its exposure.

- A corporate insider can use an equity swap to reduce exposure to his company by paying the return on the company's stock and receiving the return on a diversified portfolio benchmark or a fixed- or floating-rate interest payment.

- There can be important implications if corporate insiders use equity swaps. Insiders can reduce their exposure without giving up their voting rights, which can lead to significant agency costs. Although it is clearly necessary for investors and analysts to gauge the exposure of corporate insiders, equity swaps can make this task more difficult.

- Equity swaps pose some difficulties not faced in interest rate and currency swaps. In particular, equity swaps can generate significant cash flow problems, resulting from the fact that equity returns can be negative, meaning that one party can be required to make both sides of payments. In addition, equity swaps can involve tracking error, in which the swap returns, which are pegged to an index, do not match the returns on the actual equity portfolio that is combined with the swap.

- A party would use an interest rate swaption if it anticipates taking out a loan at a future date and entering into a swap to convert the loan from floating rate to fixed rate or vice versa. The swaption gives the party the right to enter into the swap at a specific fixed rate or better. The cost of this flexibility is the swaption premium paid up front.

- An interest rate swaption can be used to provide a means of terminating a swap at a favorable rate. A party engaged in a swap can use a swap with the opposite cash flows to effectively terminate the position. By purchasing a swaption, the party can enter into this swap at a specific rate, established in advance, or take a better rate as given in the market.

- An interest rate receiver swaption is equivalent to a call option on a bond. A party that has issued a callable bond and believes it will not call the bond can sell an interest rate receiver swaption to offset the call feature. The swaption premium received at the start offsets the higher coupon paid for the call feature on the bond. If interest rates fall enough to trigger the bond being called, the swaption will also be exercised. The party must enter into the underlying swap and can enter into an opposite swap at the market rate. The net effect is that the party ends up paying the same rate it would have paid if it had not called the bond.

- A party that has issued a noncallable bond can synthetically add a call feature by purchasing an interest rate receiver swaption. The premium paid for the swaption effectively raises the coupon rate on the bond. If rates fall sufficiently, the receiver swaption is exercised and the party enters into the underlying swap. The party then enters into a swap in the market at the market rate. The net effect is that the party pays a lower fixed rate, as though the bond had been called.

PROBLEMS

1. A company has issued floating-rate notes with a maturity of one year, an interest rate of Libor plus 125 basis points, and total face value of $50 million. The company now believes that interest rates will rise and wishes to protect itself by entering into an interest rate swap. A dealer provides a quote on a swap in which the company will pay a fixed rate 6.5% and receive Libor. Interest is paid quarterly, and the current Libor is 5%. Indicate how the company can use a swap to convert the debt to a fixed rate. Calculate the overall net payment (including the loan) by the company. Assume that all payments will be made on the basis of 90/360.

2. Assume that you manage a $100 million bond portfolio with a duration of 1.5 years. You wish to increase the duration of the bond portfolio to 3.5 years by using a swap. Assume the duration of a fixed-rate bond is 75% of its maturity.
   A. Discuss whether the swap you enter into should involve paying fixed, receiving floating or paying floating, receiving fixed.
   B. Would you prefer a four-year swap with quarterly payments or a three-year swap with semiannual payments?
   C. Determine the notional principal of the swap you would prefer.

3. A company issues a leveraged floating-rate note with a face value of $5,000,000 that pays a coupon of 2.5 times Libor. The company plans to generate a profit by selling the notes, using the proceeds to purchase a bond with a fixed coupon rate of 7% a year, and hedging the risk by entering into an appropriate swap. A swap dealer provides a quote with a fixed rate of 6% and a floating rate of Libor. Discuss whether the company should enter into a swap involving paying fixed, receiving floating or paying floating, receiving fixed. Calculate the amount of the arbitrage profit the company can earn by entering into the appropriate swap. In your answer, indicate the cash flows generated at each step. Also explain what additional risk the company is taking on by doing the swap.

4. A US company needs to raise €100,000,000. It plans to raise this money by issuing dollar-denominated bonds and using a currency swap to convert the dollars to euros. The company expects interest rates in both the United States and the eurozone to fall.
   A. Should the swap be structured with interest paid at a fixed or a floating rate?
   B. Should the swap be structured with interest received at a fixed or a floating rate?

5. A company based in the United Kingdom has a German subsidiary. The subsidiary generates €15,000,000 a year, received in equivalent semiannual installments of €7,500,000. The British company wishes to convert the euro cash flows to pounds twice a year. It plans to engage in a currency swap in order to lock in the exchange rate at which it can convert the euros to pounds. The current exchange rate is €1.5/£. The fixed rate on a plain vanilla currency swap in pounds is 7.5% per year, and the fixed rate on a plain vanilla currency swap in euros is 6.5% per year.
   A. Determine the notional principals in euros and pounds for a swap with semiannual payments that will help achieve the objective.
   B. Determine the semiannual cash flows from this swap.

6. A portfolio has a total market value of $105,000,000. The portfolio is allocated as follows: $65,000,000 is invested in a broadly diversified portfolio of domestic stocks, and

Practice Problems and Solutions: 1–9 taken from *Analysis of Derivatives for the Chartered Financial Analyst® Program*, by Don M. Chance, CFA. © 2003 CFA Institute. All other problems and solutions © CFA Institute. All rights reserved.

$40,000,000 is invested in the stock of the JK Corporation. The portfolio manager wishes to reduce exposure to JK stock by $30,000,000. The manager plans to achieve this objective by entering into a three-year equity swap using the S&P 500. Assume that settlement is made at the end of each year. Also assume that after one year the return on JK stock is 4% and the return on the S&P 500 market index is −3%.

    A. Explain the structure of the equity swap.

    B. Calculate the net cash flow for the swap at the end of one year.

7. The LKS Company is a US-based mutual fund company that manages a global portfolio 80% invested in domestic stocks and 20% invested in international stocks. The international component mimics the MSCI EAFE Index. The total market value of the portfolio is $750,000,000. The fund manager wishes to reduce the allocation to domestic stocks to 70% and increase the international allocation to 30%. The manager plans to achieve this objective by entering into a two-year equity swap using the Russell 3000 and the EAFE Index. Assume that settlement is made at the end of the first year. Also assume that after one year, the return on the Russell 3000 market index is 5% and the return on the EAFE Index is 6%.

    A. Explain the structure of the equity swap.

    B. Calculate the net cash flow for the swap at the end of one year.

8. A diversified portfolio with a market value of $800,000,000 currently has the following allocations:

Equity	80%	$640,000,000
Bonds	20%	$160,000,000

The equity portion of the portfolio is allocated as follows:

US large-cap stocks	70%	$448,000,000
International stocks	30%	$192,000,000

The bond portion of the portfolio is allocated as follows:

US government bonds	80%	$128,000,000
US corporate bonds	20%	$32,000,000

The portfolio manager wishes to change the overall allocation of the portfolio to 75% equity and 25% bonds. Within the equity category, the new allocation is to be 75% US large cap and 25% international stocks. In the bond category, the new allocation is to be 75% US government bonds and 25% US corporate bonds. The manager wants to use four-year swaps to achieve the desired allocations, with settlements at the end of each year. Assume that the counterparty payments or receipts are tied to Libor. Use generic stock or bond indices where appropriate. Indicate how the manager can use swaps to achieve the desired allocations. Construct the most efficient overall swap, in which all equivalent but opposite Libor payments are consolidated.

9. A company plans to borrow $20,000,000 in two years. The loan will be for three years and pay a floating interest rate of Libor with interest payments made every quarter. The company expects interest rates to rise in future years and thus is certain to swap the loan into a fixed-rate loan. In order to ensure that it can lock in an attractive rate, the company plans to purchase a payer swaption expiring in two years, with an exercise rate of 5% a year. The cost of the swaption is $250,000, and the settlement dates coincide with the interest payment dates for the original loan. Assume Libor at the beginning of the settlement period is 6.5% a year.

A. Calculate the net cash flows on the first settlement date if FS(2,5) is above the exercise rate.

B. Calculate the net cash flows on the first settlement date if FS(2,5) is below the exercise rate.

The following information relates to Questions 10–14 and is based on the readings on Risk Management Applications of Derivatives

Catherine Gide is the risk management director of the Millau Corporation, a large, diversified, French multinational corporation with subsidiaries in Japan, the United States, and Switzerland. One of Gide's primary responsibilities is to manage Millau's currency exposure. She has the flexibility to take tactical positions in foreign exchange markets if these positions are justified by her research. Gide and her assistant, Albert Darc, are meeting to discuss how best to deal with Millau's currency exposure over the next 12 months.

Specifically, Gide is concerned about the following:

1. Millau has just sold a Japanese subsidiary for 65 billion yen (JPY65,000,000,000). Because of an impending tax law change, Gide wishes to wait six months before repatriating these funds. Gide plans to invest the sale proceeds in six-month Japanese government securities and hedge the currency risk by using forward contracts. Gide's research indicates that the yen will depreciate against the euro (EUR) over the next six months. Darc has gathered the exchange rate and interest rate information given in Exhibit 1. The day-count convention is 30/360.

2. Millau has a contract to deliver computerized machine tools to a US buyer in three months. A payment of 50 million US dollars (USD50,000,000) is due from the buyer at that time. Gide is concerned about the dollar weakening relative to the euro. She plans to use options to hedge this currency exposure. Specifically, Gide expects the US dollar to weaken to 1.2250USD/EUR in the next three months. Euro options quotations are given in Exhibit 2. All options are European-style and expire in three months.

3. Darc says to Gide:

   "I believe the volatility of the USD/EUR exchange rate will soon increase by more than the market expects. We may be able to profit from this volatility increase by buying an equal number of at-the-money call and put options on the euro at the same strike price and expiration date."

4. Millau needs 100 million Swiss francs (CHF100,000,000) for a period of one year. Millau can issue at par a 2.8% one-year euro-denominated note with semiannual coupons and swap the proceeds into Swiss francs. The euro swap fixed rate is 2.3% and the Swiss franc swap fixed rate is 0.8%.

   Darc tells Gide that he expects interest rates in both the euro currency zone and Switzerland to rise in the near future. Exchange rate and interest rate information is given in Exhibit 1.

EXHIBIT 1   Exchange Rate and Interest Rate Information

Currency Exchange Rates	Spot	3-Month Forward	6-Month Forward	1-Year Forward
US dollars per euro (USD/EUR)	1.1930	1.1970	1.2030	1.2140
Japanese yen per euro (JPY/EUR)	133.83	133.14	132.46	131.13
Swiss francs per euro (CHF/EUR)	1.5540	1.5490	1.5440	1.5340

Annualized Risk-Free Interest Rates (%)	1 Month	3 Month	6 Month	1 Year
Euro area	2.110	2.120	2.130	2.150
United States	3.340	3.560	3.770	3.990
Japan	0.040	0.056	0.066	0.090
Switzerland	0.730	0.750	0.760	0.780

EXHIBIT 2   Euro Options Quotations (Options Expire in 3 Months)

Strike (USD/EUR)	Calls on Euro (USD/EUR)	Puts on Euro (USD/EUR)
1.1800	0.0275	0.0125
1.1900	0.0216	0.0161
1.2000	0.0169	0.0211
1.2100	0.0127	0.0278

10. If Gide uses a six-month forward currency contract to convert the yen received from the sale of the Japanese subsidiary into euros, the total amount Millau will receive is *closest* to:
    A. EUR490,714,000.
    B. EUR490,876,000.
    C. EUR491,038,000.

11. If Gide uses a six-month forward currency contract to convert the yen received from the sale of the Japanese subsidiary into euros, the annualized return in euros that Millau will realize is *closest* to:
    A. 0.066%.
    B. 2.130%.
    C. 2.196%.

12. Darc's statement to Gide (in concern #3) about the option strategy to use in order to profit from a volatility increase of the euro/US dollar exchange rate is:
    A. correct.
    B. incorrect, because he is describing a strategy that benefits only from a weakening euro.
    C. incorrect, because he is describing a strategy that benefits from low volatility in the exchange rate.

13. If Millau issues euro-denominated debt and enters into a fixed-rate currency swap (in concern #4), which of the following *best* describes transactions between Millau and the swap counterparty in six months? Millau pays the swap counterparty:
    A. EUR740,026 and receives CHF400,000.
    B. CHF400,000 and receives EUR740,026.
    C. CHF800,000 and receives EUR900,901.

14. Based on Darc's interest rate expectations for the euro currency zone and Switzerland, Gide's *best* choice is to structure the currency swap so that Millau pays interest at a:
    A. fixed rate and receives it at a fixed rate.
    B. fixed rate and receives it at a floating rate.
    C. floating rate and receives it at a floating rate.

The following information relates to Questions 15–20 and is based on the readings on Risk Management Applications of Derivatives

Hadley Elbridge, managing director for Humber Wealth Managers, LLC, is concerned about the risk level of a client's equity portfolio. The client, Pat Cassidy, has 60% of this portfolio invested in two equity positions: Hop Industries and Sure Securities. Cassidy refuses to sell his shares in either company, but has agreed to use option strategies to manage these concentrated equity positions. Elbridge recommends either a collar strategy or a protective put strategy on the Hop position, and a covered call strategy on the Sure position. The options available to construct the positions are shown in Exhibit 1.

EXHIBIT 1　　Equity Positions and Options Available

Stock	Shares	Stock Price	Options	Option Price
Hop	375,000	$26.20	September 25.00 put	$0.80
			September 27.50 call	$0.65
Sure	300,000	$34.00	September 32.50 put	$0.85
			September 35.00 call	$1.20

Cassidy makes the following comments:

Comment #1　"The Hop protective put position provides a maximum per share loss of $2.00 and a breakeven underlying price at expiration of $27.00."

Comment #2　"The Sure covered call position provides a maximum per share gain of $2.20 and a breakeven underlying price at expiration of $32.80."

Comment #3　"The general shape of a profit-and-loss graph for the protective put closely resembles the general shape of the graph for another common option position."

Elbridge also investigates whether a privately negotiated equity swap could be used to reduce the risk of the Hop and Sure holdings. A swap dealer offers Elbridge the following:

- The dealer will receive the return on 250,000 shares of Hop and 200,000 shares of Sure from Cassidy.
- The dealer will pay Cassidy the return on an equivalent dollar amount on the Russell 3000 Index.

The dealer demonstrates the quarterly cash flows of this transaction under the assumptions that Hop is up 2%, Sure is up 4%, and the Russell 3000 is up 5% for the quarter.

The remaining 40% of Cassidy's equity portfolio is invested in a diversified portfolio of equities valued at $13,350,000. Elbridge believes this portfolio is too risky, so he recommends lowering the beta of this portfolio from its current level of 1.20 to a target beta of 0.80. To accomplish this, he will use a two-month futures contract with a price (including multiplier) of $275,000 and a beta of 0.97.

15. Disregarding the initial cost of the Hop collar strategy, the value per share of the strategy at expiration with the stock at $26.90 is:
    A. $26.05.
    B. $26.20.
    C. $26.90.

16. Cassidy's Comments #1 and #2 about the Hop protective put and Sure covered call positions, respectively, are:

	Protective Put	Covered Call
A.	Correct	Correct
B.	Correct	Incorrect
C.	Incorrect	Incorrect

17. The general shape of the profit-and-loss graph in Cassidy's Comment #3 is *most* similar to the general shape of the profit-and-loss graph for:
    A. buying a call.
    B. selling a call.
    C. buying a put.

18. If an options dealer takes the other side of the Sure option position, the dealer's initial option delta and hedging transaction, respectively, will be:

	Dealer's Initial Option Delta	Dealer's Hedging Transaction
A.	Negative	Buy the underlying
B.	Positive	Buy the underlying
C.	Positive	Sell the underlying

19. What is the payoff to Cassidy in the equity swap example?
    A. −$269,500.
    B. $264,500.
    C. $269,500.

20. To achieve the target beta on Cassidy's diversified stock portfolio, Elbridge would sell the following number of futures contracts (rounded to the nearest whole contract):
    A. 13.
    B. 20.
    C. 27.

Questions 21 through 26 relate to the Westfield Tool Company

The Westfield Machine Tool and Die Company (WMTC) is a US-based manufacturer of cutting tools that operates production plants in the United States and Spain. WMTC's CEO has received an economic report forecasting that interest rates in the future will likely increase worldwide. He has asked WMTC's CFO, Yolanda Lopez, to examine ways by which different kinds of swaps could be used as a means of reducing the company's interest rate and currency risks.

Lopez has identified the following areas where swaps might be an attractive tool for managing risk:

- WMTC's employee pension plan portfolio
- WMTC's existing five-year bank loan
- Foreign exchange risk associated with cash flows repatriated from the operations in Spain
- New debt issue associated with upcoming expansion projects

Information regarding WMTC's pension plan portfolio is shown in Exhibit 1. Within the WMTC pension plan portfolio, the allocation within equities is heavily weighted towards the company's own stock. WMTC would like to retain these shares for corporate control purposes.

EXHIBIT 1   Pension Plan Portfolio of Westfield Machine
Tool Company (in millions of US dollars)

Equities	
Diversified Equities	$200
WMTC Common Stock	$400
Equities Total	$600
Fixed Income (Bonds)*	
Treasuries	$200
Corporates	$300
Fixed Income Total	$500
Bond Portfolio Duration	6 years
Total Portfolio Value	$1,100

*All bonds are fixed rate, and pay interest semiannually and on the same date.

Lopez recommends the allocation to WMTC equity be reduced to 20% of the overall equity portfolio. Lopez determines that WTMC can achieve this reallocation objective by executing an equity swap that would enable it to alter the allocation more easily and less expensively than by executing transactions in the underlying securities. Furthermore, using the equity swap would allow WMTC to retain the company shares held in the WMTC pension portfolio.

Lopez also recommends that WMTC reduce the duration of the bond portfolio by 50%. She states that, in order to achieve this duration target, WMTC should use a 6-year interest rate swap with semiannual payments. Lopez estimates the duration of the swap's fixed payments to be 75% of the swap maturity.

Lopez is also concerned about WMTC's five-year variable rate loan given the forecast of rising interest rates. Additionally, Lopez would like to use a currency swap to lock in the exchange rate when WMTC repatriates Euro cash flows from Spain into US dollars over the next two years. Additional pertinent facts regarding WMTC's existing debt obligation and cash flows from Spain are provided in Exhibit 2.

EXHIBIT 2   Relevant Debt and Cash Flow Information

Debt:	Five-year variable rate loan. Principal amount: $10,000,000. Rate: Libor + 200 basis points, paid semiannually, reset every six months. Loan rate was reset today at a Libor of 5%.
Cash Flows:	Estimated €12 million annually to be repatriated to US from operations in Spain, in equal semiannual installments. Current spot exchange rate: 1.4 USD/EUR

To hedge the interest rate risk on the five-year variable rate loan, Lopez recommends that WMTC enter into a contract with Swap Traders International (STI), who offers an interest rate swap with a notional principal of $10 million that provides a fixed rate of 6% in exchange for Libor, with semiannual payments.

To hedge the currency risk associated with the cash flows to be repatriated from its operations in Spain. Lopez recommends that WMTC enter into a currency swap with semiannual payments, where the fixed swap rate in Euros is 4.5%, and the fixed swap rate in US dollars is 5.00%.

WMTC also has some major expansion plans for its Spanish operations. In two years, Lopez expects that WMTC will need to raise €50 million. Lopez expects that WMTC will raise the funds using a floating interest rate loan at the prevailing Libor rate in 2 years with annual interest payments. Lopez is considering hedging the interest rate risk relating to the future borrowing, so she contacts STI, who offers a swaption expiring in 2 years with Libor as the underlying floating rate and an exercise rate of 6%.

21. Lopez will *most likely* achieve the pension plan's equity reallocation objective by entering into an equity swap whereby WMTC receives a return on:
    A. $320 million of the S&P 500 Index and pays a return on $320 million of WMTC common stock.
    B. $280 million of the S&P 500 Index and pays a return on $280 million of WMTC common stock.
    C. $280 million of WMTC common stock and pays a return on $280 million of the S&P 500 Index.

22. To achieve the target duration for the pension plan's bond portfolio, WMTC should enter into an interest rate swap with a modified duration that is:
    A. negative, requiring WTMC to make fixed-rate payments and receive floating-rate payments.
    B. negative, requiring WTMC to make floating-rate payments and receive fixed-rate payments.
    C. positive, requiring WTMC to make fixed-rate payments and receive floating-rate payments.

23. WMTC can achieve the bond portfolio duration target by using an interest rate swap with a notional principal *closest* to:
    A. $343 million.
    B. $353 million.
    C. $375 million.

24. If WMTC hedges the interest rate risk on the five-year variable rate loan by using the interest rate swap recommended by Lopez, the net interest payment at the first settlement date in six months would be *closest* to:
    A. $300,000.
    B. $400,000.
    C. $800,000.

25. If WMTC hedges the currency risk relating to the cash flows from its Spanish operations using the currency swap recommended by Lopez, WMTC would generate semiannual cash inflows from the swap *closest* to:
    A. $4.8 million.
    B. $8.4 million.
    C. $9.3 million.

26. If Lopez decides to use a swaption with STI to hedge the interest rate risk relating to the expansion loan, then Lopez should:
    A. sell a payer swaption.
    B. buy a payer swaption.
    C. buy a receiver swaption.

PART II

SOLUTIONS

CHAPTER 1

DERIVATIVE MARKETS AND INSTRUMENTS

SOLUTIONS

1. C is correct. A derivative is a financial instrument that transforms the performance of the underlying. The transformation of performance function of derivatives is what distinguishes it from mutual funds and exchange traded funds that pass through the returns of the underlying.

    A is incorrect because derivatives, in contrast to mutual funds and exchange traded funds, do not simply pass through the returns of the underlying at payout. B is incorrect because a derivative transforms rather than replicates the performance of the underlying.

2. B is correct. Over-the counter-derivatives markets are customized and mostly unregulated. As a result, over-the-counter markets are less transparent in comparison with the high degree of transparency and standardization associated with exchange-traded derivative markets.

    A is incorrect because exchange-traded derivatives are standardized, whereas over-the-counter derivatives are customized. C is incorrect because exchange-traded derivatives are characterized by a high degree of transparency because all transactions are disclosed to exchanges and regulatory agencies, whereas over-the-counter derivatives are relatively opaque.

3. C is correct. Exchanged-traded derivatives are guaranteed by a clearinghouse against default.

    A is incorrect because traded derivatives are characterized by a relatively high degree of regulation. B is incorrect because the terms of exchange-traded derivatives terms are specified by the exchange.

4. C is correct. A credit default swap (CDS) is a derivative in which the credit protection seller provides protection to the credit protection buyer against the credit risk of a separate party. CDS are classified as a contingent claim.

    A is incorrect because futures contracts are classified as forward commitments. B is incorrect because interest rate swaps are classified as forward commitments.

5. B is correct. Forward commitments represent an obligation to buy or sell the underlying asset at an agreed upon price at a future date.

   A is incorrect because the right to buy or sell the underlying asset is a characteristic of contingent claims, not forward commitments. C is incorrect because a credit default swap provides a promise to provide credit protection to the credit protection buyer in the event of a credit event such as a default or credit downgrade and is classified as a contingent claim.

6. A is correct. Options are classified as a contingent claim which provides payoffs that are non-linearly related to the performance of the underlying.

   B is incorrect because forwards are classified as a forward commitment, which provides payoffs that are linearly related to the performance of the underlying. C is incorrect because interest-rate swaps are classified as a forward commitment, which provides payoffs that are linearly related to the performance of the underlying.

7. A is correct. An interest rate swap is defined as a derivative in which two parties agree to exchange a series of cash flows: One set of cash flows is variable, and the other set can be variable or fixed.

   B is incorrect because a credit derivative is a derivative contract in which the credit protection seller provides protection to the credit protection buyer. C is incorrect because a call option gives the buyer the right to purchase the underlying from the seller.

8. C is correct. Interest rate swaps and forwards are over-the-counter contracts that are privately negotiated and are both subject to default. Futures contracts are traded on an exchange, which provides a credit guarantee and protection against default.

   A is incorrect because futures are exchange-traded contracts which provide daily settlement of gains and losses and a credit guarantee by the exchange through its clearinghouse. B is incorrect because futures are exchange-traded contracts which provide daily settlement of gains and losses and a credit guarantee by the exchange through its clearinghouse.

9. B is correct. The buyer of the option pays the option premium to the seller of the option at the initiation of the contract. The option premium represents the value of the option, whereas futures and forwards have a value of zero at the initiation of the contract.

   A is incorrect because no money changes hands between parties at the initiation of the futures contract, thus the value of the futures contract is zero at initiation. C is incorrect because no money changes hands between parties at the initiation of the forward contract, thus the value of the forward contract is zero at initiation.

10. B is correct. A credit derivative is a derivative contract in which the credit protection seller provides protection to the credit protection buyer against the credit risk of a third party.

    A is incorrect because the clearinghouse provides a credit guarantee to both the buyer and the seller of a futures contract, whereas a credit derivative is between two parties, in which the credit protection seller provides a credit guarantee to the credit protection buyer. C is incorrect because futures contracts require that both the buyer and the seller of the futures contract provide a cash deposit for a portion of the futures transaction into a margin account, often referred to as a performance bond or good faith deposit.

11. A is correct. Derivative markets typically have greater liquidity than the underlying spot market as a result of the lower capital required to trade derivatives compared with the underlying. Derivatives also have lower transaction costs and lower capital requirements than the underlying.

    B is incorrect because transaction costs for derivatives are lower than the underlying spot market. C is incorrect because derivatives markets have lower capital requirements than the underlying spot market.

12. B is correct. One of the benefits of derivative markets is that derivatives create trading strategies not otherwise possible in the underlying spot market, thus providing opportunities for more effective risk management than simply replicating the payoff of the underlying.

   A is incorrect because effective risk management is one of the primary purposes associated with derivative markets. C is incorrect because one of the operational advantages associated with derivatives is that it is easier to go short compared to the underlying spot market.

13. A is correct. The benefits of derivatives, such as low transaction costs, low capital requirements, use of leverage, and the ease in which participants can go short, also can result in excessive speculative trading. These activities can lead to defaults on the part of speculators and creditors.

   B is incorrect because arbitrage activities tend to bring about a convergence of prices to intrinsic value. C is incorrect because asymmetric performance is not itself destabilizing.

14. C is correct. The law of one price occurs when market participants engage in arbitrage activities so that identical assets sell for the same price in different markets.

   A is incorrect because the law of one price refers to identical assets. B is incorrect because it refers to arbitrage not the law of one price.

15. A is correct. Arbitrage opportunities exist when the same asset or two equivalent combinations of assets that produce the same results sell for different prices. When this situation occurs, market participants would buy the asset in the cheaper market and simultaneously sell it in the more expensive market, thus earning a riskless arbitrage profit without committing any capital.

   B is incorrect because it is not the definition of an arbitrage opportunity. C is incorrect because it is not the definition of an arbitrage opportunity.

CHAPTER 2

BASICS OF DERIVATIVE PRICING AND VALUATION

SOLUTIONS

1. A is correct. An illiquid position is a limit to arbitrage because it may be difficult to realize gains of an illiquid offsetting position. A significant opportunity arises from a sufficiently large price differential or a small price differential that can be employed on a very large scale.

2. A is correct. Some arbitrage opportunities represent such small price discrepancies that they are only worth exploiting if the transaction costs are low. An arbitrage opportunity may require short-selling assets at costs that eliminate any profit potential. If the law of one price holds, there is no arbitrage opportunity.

3. C is correct. Arbitrage is a type of transaction undertaken when two assets or portfolios produce identical results but sell for different prices. A trader buys the asset or portfolio with the lower price and sells the asset or portfolio with the higher price, generating a net inflow of funds at the start of the holding period. Because the two assets or portfolios produce identical results, a long position in one and short position in the other means that at the end of the holding period, the payoffs offset. Therefore, there is no money gained or lost at the end of the holding period, so there is no risk.

4. B is correct. The forward price is agreed upon at the start of the contract and is the fixed price at which the underlying will be purchased (or sold) at expiration. Payment is made at expiration. The value of the forward contract may change over time, but the forward price does not change.

5. C is correct. The price of a forward contract is a contractually fixed price, established at initiation, at which the underlying will be purchased (or sold) at expiration. The value of a forward contract at initiation is zero; therefore, the forward price is greater than the value of the forward contract at initiation.

6. B is correct. The value of the forward contract, unlike its price, will adjust as market conditions change. The forward price is fixed at initiation.

7. A is correct. When a forward contract expires, if the spot price is higher than the forward price, the long party profits from paying the lower forward price for the underlying. Therefore, the forward contract has a positive value to the long party and a negative value to the short party. However, if the forward price is higher than the spot price, the short party profits from receiving the higher forward price (the contract value is positive to the short party and negative to the long party).

8. B is correct. At initiation, the forward price is the future value of the spot price (spot price compounded at the risk-free rate over the life of the contract). If the forward price were set to the spot price or the present value of the spot price, it would be possible for one side to earn an arbitrage profit by selling the asset and investing the proceeds until contract expiration.

9. A is correct. The forward price of each stock is found by compounding the spot price by the risk-free rate for the period and then subtracting the future value of any benefits and adding the future value of any costs. In the absence of any benefits or costs, the one-year forward prices of BWQ and ZER should be equal. After subtracting the benefits related to BWQ, the one-year forward price of BWQ is lower than the one-year forward price of ZER.

10. A is correct. An asset's forward price is increased by the future value of any costs and decreased by the future value of any benefits: $F_0(T) = S_0(1 + r)^T - (\gamma - \theta)(1 + r)^T$. If the net cost of carry (benefits less costs) is positive, the forward price is lower than if the net cost of carry was zero.

11. C is correct. When a commodity's storage costs exceed its convenience yield benefits, the net cost of carry (benefits less costs) is negative. Subtracting this negative amount from the spot price compounded at the risk-free rate results in an addition to the compounded spot price. The result is a commodity forward price which is higher than the spot price compounded. The commodity's forward price is less than the spot price compounded when the convenience yield benefits exceed the storage costs and the commodity's forward price is the same as the spot price compounded when the costs equal the benefits.

12. C is correct. The convenience yield is a benefit of holding the asset and generally exists when a commodity is in short supply. The future value of the convenience yield is subtracted from the compounded spot price and reduces the commodity's forward price relative to it spot price. The opportunity cost is the risk-free rate. In the absence of carry costs, the forward price is the spot price compounded at the risk-free rate and will exceed the spot price. Dividends are benefits that reduce the forward price but the lack of dividends has no effect on the spot price relative to the forward price of a commodity in short supply.

13. B is correct. When interest rates are constant, forwards and futures will likely have the same prices. The price differential will vary with the volatility of interest rates. In addition, if futures prices and interest rates are uncorrelated, forward and futures prices will be the same. If futures prices are positively correlated with interest rates, futures contracts are more desirable to holders of long positions than are forwards. This is because rising prices lead to future profits that are reinvested in periods of rising interest rates, and falling prices lead to losses that occur in periods of falling interest rates. If futures prices are negatively correlated with interest rates, futures contracts are less desirable to holders of long positions than are forwards. The more desirable contract will tend to have the higher price.

14. C is correct. Futures contracts are marked-to-market on a daily basis. The accumulated gains and losses from the previous day's trading session are deducted from the accounts of those holding losing positions and transferred to the accounts of those holding winning

positions. Futures contracts trade on an exchange, forward contracts are over-the-counter transactions. Typically both forward and futures contracts are initiated at a zero value.

15. A is correct. If futures prices and interest rates are negatively correlated, forwards are more desirable to holders of long positions than are futures. This is because rising prices lead to futures profits that are reinvested in periods of falling interest rates. It is better to receive all of the cash at expiration under such conditions. If futures prices and interest rates are uncorrelated, forward and futures prices will be the same. If futures prices are positively correlated with interest rates, futures contracts are more desirable to holders of long positions than are forwards.

16. B is correct. Valuation of the swap during its life appeals to replication and the principle of arbitrage. Valuation consists of reproducing the remaining payments on the swap with other transactions. The value of that replication strategy is the value of the swap. The swap price is typically set such that the swap contract has a value of zero at initiation. The value of a swap contract will change during the life of the contract as the value of the underlying changes in value.

17. C is correct. Replication is the key to pricing a swap. The swap price is determined at initiation by replication. The value (not the price) of the swap is typically zero at initiation and the fixed swap price is typically determined such that the value of the swap will be zero at initiation.

18. B is correct. The principal of replication articulates that the valuation of a swap is the present value of all the net cash flow payments from the swap, not simply the present value of the fixed payments of the swap or the present value of the underlying at the end of the contract.

19. B is correct. If the underlying has a value equal to the exercise price at expiration, both options will have zero value since they both have the same exercise price. For example, if the exercise price is $25 and at expiration the underlying price is $25, both the call option and the put option will have a value of zero. The value of an option cannot fall below zero. The holder of an option is not obligated to exercise the option; therefore, the options each have a minimum value of zero. If the call has a positive value, the put, by definition, must have a zero value and vice versa. Both cannot have a positive value.

20. C is correct. A European put option will be valuable at expiration if the exercise price is greater than the underlying price. The holder can put (deliver) the underlying and receive the exercise price which is higher than the spot price. A European put option would be worthless if the exercise price was equal to or less than the underlying price.

21. B is correct. The value of a European call option at expiration is the greater of zero or the value of the underlying minus the exercise price.

22. B is correct. A European call option with two months until expiration will typically have positive time value, where time value reflects the value of the uncertainty that arises from the volatility in the underlying. The call option has a zero exercise value if the spot price is below the exercise price. The exercise value of a European call option is $Max(0, S_t - X)$, where S_t is the current spot price at time t and X is the exercise price.

23. A is correct. When the price of the underlying is below the exercise price for a put, the option is said to be in-the-money. If the price of the underlying is the same as the exercise price, the put is at-the-money and if it is above the exercise price, the put is out-of-the-money.

24. A is correct. An in-the-money European put option decreases in value with an increase in the risk-free rate. A higher risk-free rate reduces the present value of any proceeds received on exercise.

25. A is correct. The value of a European call option is inversely related to the exercise price. A lower exercise price means there are more potential outcomes at which the call expires in-the-money. The option value will be greater the lower the exercise price. For a higher exercise price, the opposite is true. Both the time to expiration and the volatility of the underlying are directly (positively) related to the value of a European call option.

26. B is correct. The value of a European call option is inversely related to the exercise price and directly related to the time to expiration. Option 1 and Option 2 have the same exercise price; however, Option 2 has a longer time to expiration. Consequently, Option 2 would likely have a higher value than Option 1. Option 2 and Option 3 have the same time to expiration; however, Option 2 has a lower exercise price. Thus, Option 2 would likely have a higher value than Option 3.

27. B is correct. The value of a European put option can be either directly or indirectly related to time to expiration. The direct effect is more common, but the inverse effect can prevail the longer the time to expiration, the higher the risk-free rate, and the deeper in-the-money is the put. The value of a European put option is directly related to the exercise price and the volatility of the underlying.

28. B is correct. Prior to expiration, the lowest value of a European put is the greater of zero or the present value of the exercise price minus the value of the underlying.

29. C is correct. Payments, such as dividends, reduce the value of the underlying which increases the value of a European put option. Carrying costs reduce the value of a European put option. An increase in the risk-free interest rate may decrease the value of a European put option.

30. A is correct. A long bond can be synthetically created by combining a long asset, a long put, and a short call. A fiduciary call is created by combining a long call with a risk free bond. A protective put is created by combining a long asset with a long put.

31. B is correct. According to put–call parity, a synthetic call can be constructed by combining a long asset, long put, and short bond positions.

32. C is correct. The actual probabilities of the up and down moves in the underlying do not appear in the binomial option pricing model, only the pseudo or "risk-neutral" probabilities. Both the spot price of the underlying and two possible prices one period later are required by the binomial option pricing model.

33. C is correct. Prior to expiration, an American call option will typically have a value in the market that is greater than its exercise value. Although the American option is at-the-money and therefore has an exercise value of zero, the time value of the call option would likely lead to the option having a positive market value.

34. B is correct. At expiration, the values of American and European call options are effectively the same; both are worth the greater of zero and the exercise value.

35. A is correct. When a dividend is declared, an American call option will have a higher value than a European call option because an American call option holder can exercise early to capture the value of the dividend. At expiration, both types of call options are worth the greater of zero and the exercise value. A change in the risk-free rate does not affect the relative values of American and European call options.

36. A is correct. Put–call forward parity demonstrates that the outcome of a protective put with a forward contract (long put, long risk-free bond, long forward contract) equals the outcome of a fiduciary call (long call, long risk-free bond). The outcome of a protective put with a forward contract is also equal to the outcome of a protective put with an asset (long put, long asset).

CHAPTER 3

PRICING AND VALUATION OF FORWARD COMMITMENTS

SOLUTIONS

1. B is correct.

    The no-arbitrage futures price is equal to the following:

    $$F_0(T) = \text{FV}_{0,T}(T)[B_0(T+Y) + \text{AI}_0 - \text{PVCI}_{0,T}]$$
    $$F_0(T) = (1 + 0.003)^{0.25}(112.00 + 0.08 - 0)$$
    $$F_0(T) = (1 + 0.003)^{0.25}(112.08) = 112.1640$$

    The adjusted price of the futures contract is equal to the conversion factor multiplied by the quoted futures price:

    $$F_0(T) = \text{CF}(T)\text{QF}_0(T)$$
    $$F_0(T) = (0.90)(125) = 112.50$$

    Adding the accrued interest of 0.20 in three months (futures contract expiration) to the adjusted price of the futures contract gives a total price of 112.70.

    This difference means that the futures contract is overpriced by $112.70 - 112.1640 = 0.5360$. The available arbitrage profit is the present value of this difference: $0.5360/(1.003)^{0.25} = 0.5356$.

2. B is correct. The no-arbitrage futures price is

    $$F_0(T) = S_0 e^{(r_c - \gamma)T}$$
    $$F_0(T) = 16{,}080 e^{(0.002996 - 0.011)(3/12)} = 16{,}047.68$$

3. A is correct. The value of Troubadour's euro/JGB forward position is calculated as

    $$V_t(T) = \text{PV}_{t,T}[F_t(T) - F_0(T)]$$
    $$V_t(T) = (100.05 - 100.20)/(1 + 0.0030)^{2/12} = -0.149925 \text{ (per ¥100 par value)}$$

Therefore, the value of Troubadour's forward position is

$$V_t(T) = -\frac{0.149925}{100}(\yen100{,}000{,}000) = -\yen149{,}925$$

4. C is correct. The current no-arbitrage price of the forward contract is

$$F_t(\yen/\$, T) = S_t(\yen/\$)\text{FV}_{\yen,t,T}(1)/\text{FV}_{\$,t,T}(1)$$
$$F_t(\yen/\$, T) = \yen112.00(1 - 0.002)^{0.25}/(1 + 0.003)^{0.25} = \yen111.8602$$

Therefore, the value of Troubadour's position in the $\yen/\$$ forward contract, on a per dollar basis, is

$$V_t(T) = \text{PV}_{\yen,t,T}[F_0(\yen/\$, T) - F_t(\yen/\$, T)]$$
$$= (112.10 - 111.8602)/(1 - 0.002)^{0.25} = \yen0.239963 \text{ per } \$1$$

Troubadour's position is a short position of $\$1{,}000{,}000$, so the short position has a positive value of $(\yen0.239963/\$) \times \$1{,}000{,}000 = \yen239{,}963$ because the forward rate has fallen since the contract initiation.

5. A is correct. The carry arbitrage model price of the forward contract is

$$\text{FV}(S_0) = S_0(1 + r)^T = \$250(1 + 0.003)^{0.75} = \$250.562289$$

The market price of the TSI forward contract is $\$250.562289$. A carry or reverse carry arbitrage opportunity does not exist because the market price of the forward contract is equal to the carry arbitrage model price.

6. B is correct. From the perspective of the long position, the forward value is equal to the present value of the difference in forward prices:

$$V_t(T) = \text{PV}_{t,T}[F_t(T) - F_0(T)],$$

where $F_t(T) = \text{FV}_{t,T}(S_t + \theta_t - \gamma_t)$.

All else equal, an increase in the risk-free rate before contract expiration would cause the forward price, $F_t(T)$, to increase. This increase in the forward price would cause the value of the TSI forward contract, from the perspective of the short, to decrease. Therefore, an increase in the risk-free rate would lead to a loss on the short position in the TSI forward contract.

7. C is correct. The no-arbitrage price of the forward contract, three months after contract initiation, is

$$F_{0.25}(T) = \text{FV}_{0.25,T}(S_{0.25} + \theta_{0.25} - \gamma_{0.25})$$
$$F_{0.25(T)} = [\$245 + 0 - \$1.50/(1 + 0.00325)^{(0.5 - 0.25)}]$$
$$(1 + 0.00325)^{(0.75 - 0.25)} = \$243.8966$$

Therefore, from the perspective of the long, the value of the TSI forward contract is

$$V_{0.25}(T) = \text{PV}_{0.25,T}[F_{0.25}(T) - F_0(T)]$$
$$V_{0.25}(T) = (\$243.8966 - \$250.562289)/(1 + 0.00325)^{0.75 - 0.25} = -\$6.6549$$

   Because Troubadour is short the TSI forward contract, the value of his position is a gain of $6.6549.

8. C is correct. The swap pricing equation is

$$r_{FIX} = \frac{1 - PV_{0,t_n}(1)}{\sum_{i=1}^{n} PV_{0,t_i}(1)}$$

   That is, the fixed swap rate is equal to 1 minus the final present value factor (in this case, Year 3) divided by the sum of the present values (in this case, the sum of Years 1, 2, and 3). The sum of present values for Years 1, 2, and 3 is calculated as

$$\sum_{i=1}^{n} PV_{0,t_i}(1) = 0.990099 + 0.977876 + 0.965136 = 2.933111$$

   Thus, the fixed-swap rate is calculated as

$$r_{FIX} = \frac{1 - 0.965136}{2.933111} = 0.01189 \text{ or } 1.19\%$$

9. B is correct. The value of a swap from the perspective of the receive-fixed party is calculated as

$$V = NA(FS_0 - FS_t) \sum_{i=1}^{n'} PV_{t,t_i}$$

   The swap has two years remaining until expiration. The sum of the present values for Years 1 and 2 is

$$\sum_{i=1}^{n'} PV_{t,t_i} = 00990099 + 0.977876 = 1.967975$$

   Given the current equilibrium two-year swap rate of 1.00% and the fixed swap rate at initiation of 3.00%, the swap value per dollar notional is calculated as

$$V = (0.03 - 0.01)1.967975 = 0.0393595$$

   The current value of the swap, from the perspective of the receive-fixed party, is $50,000,000 \times 0.0393595 = \$1,967,975$.

   From the perspective of the bank, as the receive-floating party, the value of the swap is $-\$1,967,975$.

10. C is correct. The equilibrium swap fixed rate for yen is calculated as

$$\hat{r}_{FIX,JPY} = \frac{1 - PV_{0,t_4,JPY}(1)}{\sum_{i=1}^{4} PV_{0,t_4,JPY}(1)}$$

The yen present value factors are calculated as

$$PV_{0,t_i}(1) = \frac{1}{1 + r_{Spot_i}\left(\dfrac{NAD_i}{NTD}\right)}$$

90-day PV factor = 1/[1 + 0.0005(90/360)] = 0.999875.
180-day PV factor = 1/[1 + 0.0010(180/360)] = 0.999500.
270-day PV factor = 1/[1 + 0.0015(270/360)] = 0.998876.
360-day PV factor = 1/[1 + 0.0025(360/360)] = 0.997506.

Sum of present value factors = 3.995757.
Therefore, the yen periodic rate is calculated as

$$\hat{r}_{FIX,JPY} = \frac{1 - 0.997506}{3.995757} = 0.000624 \text{ or } 0.0624\%$$

The annualized rate is (360/90) times the periodic rate of 0.0624%, or 0.2496%.

11. B is correct. The value of an equity swap is calculated as

$$V_t = FB_t(C_0) - \left(\frac{S_t}{S_{t-}}\right)NA_E$$

The swap was initiated six months ago, so the first reset has not yet passed; thus, there are five remaining cash flows for this equity swap. The fair value of the swap is determined by comparing the present value of the implied fixed-rate bond with the return on the equity index. The fixed swap rate of 2.00%, the swap notional amount of $20,000,000, and the present value factors in Exhibit 5 result in a present value of the implied fixed-rate bond's cash flows of $19,818,677:

Date (in years)	PV Factors	Fixed Cash Flow	PV (fixed cash flow)
0.5	0.998004 or 1/[1 + 0.0040(180/360)]	$400,000	$399,202
1.5	0.985222 or 1/[1 + 0.0100(540/360)]	$400,000	$394,089
2.5	0.970874 or 1/[1 + 0.0120(900/360)]	$400,000	$388,350
3.5	0.934579 or 1/[1 + 0.0200(1,260/360)]	$400,000	$373,832
4.5	0.895255 or 1/[1 + 0.0260(1,620/360)]	$20,400,000	$18,263,205
Total			$19,818,677

The value of the equity leg of the swap is calculated as $(103/100)(\$20,000,000) = \$20,600,000$.

Therefore, the fair value of the equity swap, from the perspective of the bank (receive-fixed, pay-equity party) is calculated as

$$V_t = \$19,818,677 - \$20,600,000 = -781,323$$

12. B is correct. The equity index level at which the swap's fair value would be zero can be calculated by setting the swap valuation formula equal to zero and solving for S_t:

$$0 = \text{FB}_t(C_0) - \left(\frac{S_t}{S_{t-}}\right)\text{NA}_E$$

The value of the fixed leg of the swap has a present value of $19,818,677, or 99.0934% of par value:

Date (years)	PV Factors	Fixed Cash Flow	PV (fixed cash flow)
0.5	0.998004	$400,000	$399,202
1.5	0.985222	$400,000	$394,089
2.5	0.970874	$400,000	$388,350
3.5	0.934579	$400,000	$373,832
4.5	0.895255	$20,400,000	$18,263,205
Total			$19,818,677

Treating the swap notional value as par value and substituting the present value of the fixed leg and S_0 into the equation yields

$$0 = 99.0934 - \left(\frac{S_t}{100}\right)100$$

Solving for S_t yields

$$S_t = 99.0934$$

13. A is correct. The current value of the 6×9 FRA is calculated as

$$V_g(0,h,m) = \{[\text{FRA}(g,h-g,m) - \text{FRA}(0,h,m)]t_m\}/[1 + D_g(h+m-g)t_{h+m-g}]$$

The 6×9 FRA expires six months after initiation. The bank entered into the FRA 90 days ago; thus, the FRA will expire in 90 days. To value the FRA, the first step is to compute the new FRA rate, which is the rate on Day 90 of an FRA that expires in 90 days in which the underlying is the 90-day Libor, or FRA(90,90,90):

$$\text{FRA}(g,h-g,m) = \{[1 + L_g(h-g+m)t_{h-g+m}]/[1 + L_0(h-g)t_{h-g}] - 1\}/t_m$$
$$\text{FRA}(90,90,90) = \{[1 + L_{90}(180 - 90 + 90)(180/360)]/[1 + L_{90}(180 - 90)$$
$$(90/360)] - 1\}/(90/360)$$
$$\text{FRA}(90,90,90) = \{[1 + L_{90}(180)(180/360)]/[1 + L_{90}(90)(90/360)] - 1\}/(90/360)$$

Exhibit 7 indicates that $L_{90}(180) = 0.95\%$ and $L_{90}(90) = 0.90\%$, so

$$\text{FRA}(90,90,90) = \{[1 + 0.0095(180/360)]/[1 + 0.0090(90/360)] - 1\}/(90/360)$$
$$\text{FRA}(90,90,90) = [(1.00475/1.00225) - 1](4) = 0.009978, \text{ or } 0.9978\%$$

Therefore, given the FRA rate at initiation of 0.70% and notional principal of $20 million from Exhibit 1, the current value of the forward contract is calculated as

$$V_g(0,h,m) = V_{90}(0,180,90)$$
$$V_{90}(0,180,90) = \$20,000,000[(0.009978 - 0.0070)(90/360)]/$$
$$[1 + 0.0095(180/360)].$$
$$V_{90}(0,180,90) = \$14,887.75/1.00475 = \$14,817.37.$$

14. C is correct. The no-arbitrage fixed rate on the 1×4 FRA is calculated as

$$\text{FRA}(0,h,m) = \{[1 + L_0(h + m)t_{h+m}]/[1 + L_0(h)t_h] - 1\}/t_m$$

For a 1×4 FRA, the two rates needed to compute the no-arbitrage FRA fixed rate are $L(30) = 0.75\%$ and $L(120) = 0.92\%$. Therefore, the no-arbitrage fixed rate on the 1×4 FRA rate is calculated as

$$\text{FRA}(0,30,90) = \{[1 + 0.0092(120/360)]/[1 + 0.0075(30/360)] - 1\}/(90/360).$$
$$\text{FRA}(0,30,90) = [(1.003066/1.000625) - 1]4 = 0.009761, \text{ or } 0.98\% \text{ rounded}$$

15. B is correct. The fixed rate on the 2×5 FRA is calculated as

$$\text{FRA}(0,h,m) = \{[1 + L_0(h + m)t_{h+m}]/[1 + L_0(h)t_h] - 1\}/t_m$$

For a 2×5 FRA, the two rates needed to compute the no-arbitrage FRA fixed rate are $L(60) = 0.82\%$ and $L(150) = 0.94\%$. Therefore, the no-arbitrage fixed rate on the 2×5 FRA rate is calculated as

$$\text{FRA}(0,60,90) = \{[1 + 0.0094(150/360)]/[1 + 0.0082(60/360)] - 1\}/(90/360)$$
$$\text{FRA}(0,60,90) = [(1.003917/1.001367) - 1]4 = 0.010186, \text{ or } 1.02\% \text{ rounded}$$

16. A is correct. Given a three-month US dollar Libor of 1.10% at expiration, the settlement amount for the bank as the receive-floating party is calculated as

$$\text{Settlement amount (receive floating)} = \text{NA}\{[L_h(m) - \text{FRA}(0,h,m)]t_m\}/[1 + D_h(m)t_m]$$
$$\text{Settlement amount (receive floating)} = \$20,000,000[(0.011 - 0.0070)(90/360)]/$$
$$[1 + 0.011(90/360)]$$
$$\text{Settlement amount (receive floating)} = \$20,000/1.00275 = \$19,945.15$$

Therefore, the bank will receive $19,945 (rounded) as the receive-floating party.

CHAPTER 4

VALUATION OF CONTINGENT CLAIMS

SOLUTIONS

1. A is correct. The hedge ratio requires the underlying stock and call option values for the up move and down move. $S^+ = 56$, and $S^- = 46$. $c^+ = \text{Max}(0,S^+ - X) = \text{Max}(0,56 - 50) = 6$, and $c^- = \text{Max}(0,S^- - X) = \text{Max}(0,46 - 50) = 0$. The hedge ratio is

$$h = \frac{c^+ - c^-}{S^+ - S^-} = \frac{6 - 0}{56 - 46} = \frac{6}{10} = 0.60$$

2. C is correct. For this approach, the risk-free rate is $r = 0.05$, the up factor is $u = S^+/S = 56/50 = 1.12$, and the down factor is $d = S^-/S = 46/50 = 0.92$. The risk-neutral probability of an up move is

$$\pi = [\text{FV}(1) - d]/(u - d) = (1 + r - d]/(u - d)$$
$$\pi = (1 + 0.05 - 0.92)/(1.12 - 0.92) = 0.13/0.20 = 0.65$$

3. A is correct. The call option can be estimated using the no-arbitrage approach or the expectations approach. With the no-arbitrage approach, the value of the call option is

$$c = hS + \text{PV}(-hS^- + c^-).$$
$$h = (c^+ - c^-)/(S^+ - S^-) = (6 - 0)/(56 - 46) = 0.60.$$
$$c = (0.60 \times 50) + (1/1.05) \times [(-0.60 \times 46) + 0].$$
$$c = 30 - [(1/1.05) \times 27.6] = 30 - 26.286 = 3.714.$$

Using the expectations approach, the risk-free rate is $r = 0.05$, the up factor is $u = S^+/S = 56/50 = 1.12$, and the down factor is $d = S^-/S = 46/50 = 0.92$. The value of the call option is

$$c = \text{PV} \times [\pi c^+ + (1 - \pi)c^-].$$
$$\pi = [\text{FV}(1) - d]/(u - d) = (1.05 - 0.92)/(1.12 - 0.92) = 0.65.$$
$$c = (1/1.05) \times [0.65(6) + (1 - 0.65)(0)] = (1/1.05)(3.9) = 3.714.$$

Both approaches are logically consistent and yield identical values.

4. B is correct. You should sell (write) the overpriced call option and then go long (buy) the replicating portfolio for a call option. The replicating portfolio for a call option is to buy h shares of the stock and borrow the present value of $(hS^- - c^-)$.

$$c = hS + PV(-hS^- + c^-).$$
$$h = (c^+ - c^-)/(S^+ - S^-) = (6 - 0)/(56 - 46) = 0.60.$$

For the example in this case, the value of the call option is 3.714. If the option is over-priced at, say, 4.50, you short the option and have a cash flow at Time 0 of +4.50. You buy the replicating portfolio of 0.60 shares at 50 per share (giving you a cash flow of –30) and borrow $(1/1.05) \times [(0.60 \times 46) - 0] = (1/1.05) \times 27.6 = 26.287$. Your cash flow for buying the replicating portfolio is $-30 + 26.287 = -3.713$. Your net cash flow at Time 0 is $+ 4.50 - 3.713 = 0.787$. Your net cash flow at Time 1 for either the up move or down move is zero. You have made an arbitrage profit of 0.787.

In tabular form, the cash flows are as follows:

Transaction	Time Step 0	Time Step 1 Down Occurs	Time Step 1 Up Occurs
Sell the call option	4.50	0	–6.00
Buy h shares	$-0.6 \times 50 = -30$	$0.6 \times 46 = 27.6$	$0.6 \times 56 = 33.6$
Borrow $-PV(-hS^- + c^-)$	$-(1/1.05) \times [(-0.6 \times 46) + 0]$ $= 26.287$	$-0.6 \times 46 = -27.6$	$-0.6 \times 46 = -27.6$
Net cash flow	0.787	0	0

5. A is correct. Using the expectations approach, the risk-neutral probability of an up move is

$$\pi = [FV(1) - d]/(u - d) = (1.03 - 0.800)/(1.300 - 0.800) = 0.46.$$

The terminal value calculations for the exercise values at Time Step 2 are

$$c^{++} = Max(0, u^2S - X) = Max[0, 1.30^2(38) - 40] = Max(0, 24.22) = 24.22.$$
$$c^{-+} = Max(0, udS - X) = Max[0, 1.30(0.80)(38) - 40] = Max(0, -0.48) = 0.$$
$$c^{--} = Max(0, d^2S - X) = Max[0, 0.80^2(38) - 40] = Max(0, -15.68) = 0.$$

Discounting back for two years, the value of the call option at Time Step 0 is

$$c = PV[\pi^2 c^{++} + 2\pi(1 - \pi)c^{-+} + (1 - \pi)^2 c^{--}].$$
$$c = [1/(1.03)]^2[0.46^2(24.22) + 2(0.46)(0.54)(0) + 0.54^2(0)].$$
$$c = [1/(1.03)]^2[5.1250] = 4.8308.$$

6. B is correct. Using the expectations approach, the risk-neutral probability of an up move is

$$\pi = [FV(1) - d]/(u - d) = (1.03 - 0.800)/(1.300 - 0.800) = 0.46.$$

An American-style put can be exercised early. At Time Step 1, for the up move, p^+ is 0.2517 and the put is out of the money and should not be exercised early ($X < S$, $40 < 49.4$). However, at Time Step 1, p^- is 8.4350 and the put is in the money by 9.60 ($X - S = 40 - 30.40$). So, the put is exercised early, and the value of early exercise (9.60) replaces the value of not exercising early (8.4350) in the binomial tree. The value of the put at Time Step 0 is now

$$p = PV[\pi p^+ + (1 - \pi)p^-] = [1/(1.03)][0.46(0.2517) + 0.54(9.60)] = 5.1454.$$

Following is a supplementary note regarding Exhibit 1.

The values in Exhibit 1 are calculated as follows.

At Time Step 2:

$p^{++} = \text{Max}(0, X - u^2 S) = \text{Max}[0, 40 - 1.300^2(38)] = \text{Max}(0, 40 - 64.22) = 0.$

$p^{-+} = \text{Max}(0, X - udS) = \text{Max}[0, 40 - 1.300(0.800)(38)] = \text{Max}(0, 40 - 39.52) = 0.48.$

$p^{--} = \text{Max}(0, X - d^2 S) = \text{Max}[0, 40 - 0.800^2(38)] = \text{Max}(0, 40 - 24.32) = 15.68.$

At Time Step 1:

$p^{+} = \text{PV}[\pi p^{++} + (1 - \pi)p^{-+}] = [1/(1.03)][0.46(0) + 0.54(0.48)] = 0.2517.$

$p^{-} = \text{PV}[\pi p^{-+} + (1 - \pi)p^{--}] = [1/(1.03)][0.46(0.48) + 0.54(15.68)] = 8.4350.$

At Time Step 0:

$p = \text{PV}[\pi p^{+} + (1 - \pi)p^{-}] = [1/(1.03)][0.46(0.2517) + 0.54(8.4350)] = 4.5346.$

7. C is correct. Both statements are correct. The expected future payoff is calculated using risk-neutral probabilities, and the expected payoff is discounted at the risk-free rate.

8. C is correct. Using the expectations approach, per 1 of notional value, the values of the call option at Time Step 2 are

$$c^{++} = \text{Max}(0, S^{++} - X) = \text{Max}(0, 0.050 - 0.0275) = 0.0225.$$
$$c^{+-} = \text{Max}(0, S^{+-} - X) = \text{Max}(0, 0.030 - 0.0275) = 0.0025.$$
$$c^{--} = \text{Max}(0, S^{--} - X) = \text{Max}(0, 0.010 - 0.0275) = 0.$$

At Time Step 1, the call values are

$$c^{+} = \text{PV}[\pi c^{++} + (1 - \pi)c^{+-}].$$
$$c^{+} = 0.961538[0.50(0.0225) + (1 - 0.50)(0.0025)] = 0.012019.$$
$$c^{-} = \text{PV}[\pi c^{+-} + (1 - \pi)c^{--}].$$
$$c^{-} = 0.980392[0.50(0.0025) + (1 - 0.50)(0)] = 0.001225.$$

At Time Step 0, the call option value is

$$c = \text{PV}[\pi c^{+} + (1 - \pi)c^{-}].$$
$$c = 0.970874[0.50(0.012019) + (1 - 0.50)(0.001225)] = 0.006429.$$

The value of the call option is this amount multiplied by the notional value, or $0.006429 \times 1,000,000 = 6,429$.

9. A is correct. Reason 1 is correct: A higher exercise price does lower the exercise value (payoff) at Time 2. Reason 2 is not correct because the risk-neutral probabilities are based on the paths that interest rates take, which are determined by the market and not the details of a particular option contract.

10. B is correct. Although the BSM model assumes continuous stock prices, it also assumes that stock returns are lognormally distributed (not normally distributed).

11. C is correct. The no-arbitrage approach to creating a call option involves buying Delta = $N(d_1) = 0.6217$ shares of the underlying stock and financing with $-N(d_2) = -0.5596$ shares of a risk-free bond priced at $\exp(-rt)(X) = \exp(-0.0022 \times 0.25)(55) = \$54.97$ per bond. Note that the value of this replicating portfolio is $n_S S + n_B B = 0.6217(57.03) - 0.5596(54.97) = \$4.6943$ (the value of the call option with slight rounding error).

12. B is correct. The formula for the BSM price of a put option is $p = e^{-rt}XN(-d_2) - SN(-d_1)$. $N(-d_1) = 1 - N(d_1) = 1 - 0.6217 = 0.3783$, and $N(-d_2) = 1 - N(d_2) = 1 - 0.5596 = 0.4404$.

Note that the BSM model can be represented as a portfolio of the stock $(n_S S)$ and zero-coupon bonds $(n_B B)$. For a put, the number of shares is $n_S = -N(-d_1) < 0$ and the number of bonds is $n_B = -N(d_2) > 0$. The value of the replicating portfolio is $n_S S + n_B B = -0.3783(57.03) + 0.4404(54.97) = \$2.6343$ (the value of the put option with slight rounding error). B is a risk-free bond priced at $\exp(-rt)(X) = \exp(-0.0022 \times 0.25)(55) = \$54.97$.

13. A is correct. Black's model to value a call option on a futures contract is $c = e^{-rT}[F_0(T)N(d_1) - XN(d_2)]$. The underlying F_0 is the futures price (186.73). The correct discount rate is the risk-free rate, $r = 0.39\%$.

14. B is correct. Lee is pointing out the option price's sensitivity to small changes in time. In the BSM approach, option price sensitivity to changes in time is given by the option Greek theta.

15. A is correct. The put is priced at \$7.4890 by the BSM model when using the historical volatility input of 24%. The market price is \$7.20. The BSM model overpricing suggests the implied volatility of the put must be lower than 24%.

16. C is correct. Solomon's forecast is for the three-month Libor to exceed 0.85% in six months. The correct option valuation inputs use the six-month FRA rate as the underlying, which currently has a rate of 0.75%.

17. B is correct because selling call options creates a short position in the ETF that would hedge his current long position in the ETF.

Exhibit 2 could also be used to answer the question. Solomon owns 10,000 shares of the GPX, each with a delta of +1; by definition, his portfolio delta is +10,000. A delta hedge could be implemented by selling enough calls to make the portfolio delta neutral:

$$N_H = \frac{\text{Portfolio delta}}{\text{Delta}_H} = \frac{+10,000}{+0.6232} = -16,046 \text{ calls.}$$

18. C is correct. Because the gamma of the stock position is 0 and the put gamma is always non-negative, adding a long position in put options would most likely result in a positive portfolio gamma.

Gamma is the change in delta from a small change in the stock's value. A stock position always has a delta of +1. Because the delta does not change, gamma equals 0.

The gamma of a call equals the gamma of a similar put, which can be proven using put–call parity.

CHAPTER 5

DERIVATIVES STRATEGIES

SOLUTIONS

1. C is correct. To construct a synthetic long put option, Nuñes would take a short position in IZD shares and buy a call option on IZD.

2. A is correct. Strategy 2 is a covered call, which is a combination of a long position in shares and a short call option. The breakeven point of Strategy 2 is €91.26, which represents the price per share of €93.93 minus the call premium received of €2.67 per share ($S_0 - c_0$). So, at any share price less than €91.26 at option expiration, Strategy 2 incurs a loss. If the share price of IZD at option expiration is greater than €91.26, Strategy 2 generates a gain.

3. A is correct. Strategy 3 is a covered call strategy, which is a combination of a long position in shares and a short call option. The breakeven share price for a covered call is the share price minus the call premium received, or $S_0 - c_0$. The current share price of IZD is €93.93, and the IZD April €97.50 call premium is €1.68. Thus, the breakeven underlying share price for Strategy 3 is $S_0 - c_0 = €93.93 - €1.68 = €92.25$.

4. B is correct. Strategy 4 is a protective put position, which is a combination of a long position in shares and a long put option. By purchasing the €25.00 strike put option, Nuñes would be protected from losses at QWY share prices of €25.00 or lower. Thus, the maximum loss per share from Strategy 4 would be the loss of share value from €28.49 to €25.00 (or, €3.49) plus the put premium paid for the put option of €0.50: $S_0 - X + p_0 = €28.49 - €25.00 + €0.50 = €3.99$.

5. A is correct. Strategy 5 describes a collar, which is a combination of a long position in shares, a long put option with an exercise price below the current stock price, and a short call option with an exercise price above the current stock price.

6. B is correct. Strategy 5 describes a collar, which is a combination of a long position in shares, a long put option, and a short call option. Strategy 5 would require Nuñes to buy 100 QWY shares at the current market price of €28.49 per share. In addition, she would purchase a QWY April €24.00 strike put option contract for €0.35 per share and collect €0.32 per share from writing a QWY April €31.00 strike call option. The collar offers protection against losses on the shares below the put strike price of €24.00 per share but limits upside to the call strike price of €31.00 per share. Thus, the maximum gain on the

trade, which occurs at prices of €31.00 per share or higher, is calculated as $(X_0 - S_0) - p_0 + c_0$, or $(€31.00 - €28.49) - €0.35 + €0.32 = €2.48$ per share.

7. B is correct. Strategy 6 describes a bear spread, which is a combination of a long put option and a short put option on the same underlying, where the long put has a higher strike price than the short put. In the case of Strategy 6, the April €31.00 put option would be purchased and the April €25.00 put option would be sold. The long put premium is €3.00 and the short put premium is €0.50, for a net cost of €2.50. The breakeven share price is €28.50, calculated as $X_H - (p_H - p_L) = €31.00 - (€3.00 - €0.50) = €28.50$.

8. B is correct. Strategy 7 describes a short straddle, which is a combination of a short put option and a short call option, both with the same strike price. The maximum gain is €5.76 per share, which represents the sum of the two option premiums, or $c_0 + p_0 = €2.54 + €3.22 = €5.76$. The maximum gain per share is realized if both options expire worthless, which would happen if the share price of XDF at expiration is €75.00.

9. C is correct. Nuñes would implement Strategy 8, which is a long calendar spread, if she expects the XDF share price to increase between the February and December expiration dates. This strategy provides income from the February short call premium to partially offset the cost of the December long call option. Nuñes likely expects the XDF share price to remain relatively flat between the current price €74.98 and €80 until the February call option expires, after which time she expects the share price to increase above €80. If such expectations come to fruition, the February call would expire worthless and Nuñes would realize gains on the December call option.

10. C is correct. Nuñes should recommend a long straddle, which is a combination of a long call option and a long put option, both with the same strike price. The committee's announcement is expected to cause a significant move in XDF's share price. A long straddle is appropriate because it is expected that the share price will move sharply up or down depending on the committee's decision. If the merger is approved, the share price will likely increase, leading to a gain in the long call option. If the merger is rejected, then the share price will likely decrease, leading to a gain in the long put option.

CHAPTER 6

RISK MANAGEMENT

SOLUTIONS

1. Centralized risk control systems bring all risk management activities under the responsibility of a single risk control unit. Under decentralized systems, each business unit is responsible for its own risk control. The advantages of a centralized system are that it brings risk control closer to the key decision makers in the organization and enables the organization to better manage its risk budget by recognizing the diversification embedded across business units. The decentralized approach has the advantage of placing risk control in nearer proximity to the source of risk taking. However, it has the disadvantage of not accounting for portfolio effects across units.

2. The following risk exposures should be reported as part of an Enterprise Risk Management System for Ford Motor Company:
   - *Market risks*
     - Currency risk, because expenditures and receipts denominated in nondomestic currencies create exposure to changes in exchange rates.
     - Interest rate risk, because the values of securities that Ford has invested in are subject to changes in interest rates. Also, Ford has borrowings and loans, which could be affected by interest rate changes.
     - Commodity risk, because Ford has exposure in various commodities and finished products.
   - *Credit risk*, because of financing provided to customers who have purchased Ford's vehicles on credit.
   - *Liquidity risk*, because of the possibility that Ford's funding sources may be reduced or become unavailable and Ford may then have to sell its securities at a short notice with a significant concession in price.
   - *Settlement risk*, because of Ford's investments in fixed-income instruments and derivative contracts, some of which effect settlement through the execution of bilateral agreements and involve the possibility of default by the counterparty.
   - *Political risk*, because Ford has operations in several countries. This exposes it to political risk. For example, the adoption of a restrictive policy by a non-US government regarding

payment of dividends by a subsidiary in that country to the parent company could adversely affect Ford.

3. Two types of risk that were inadequately managed were model risk and operational risk. Systematic errors in a major input of the options pricing model, implied volatility, resulted in mispricing options and trading losses. Thus model risk was inadequately managed. Furthermore, the systems and procedures at NatWest failed to prevent or detect and bring to the attention of senior management the trading losses. Thus operational risk also was not well managed.

4. Trader 1's statement is incorrect. Buyers are concerned about the transaction costs of trades as much as sellers, so a security's liquidity is highly relevant to buyers. In certain cases, such as a short position in a stock with limited float, the liquidity risk for the purchase side of a trade can be considerable.

   Trader 2's statement is incorrect. Derivatives usually do not help in managing liquidity risk because the lack of liquidity in the spot market typically passes right through to the derivatives market.

   Trader 3's statement is correct. Businesses need to take risks in areas in which they have expertise and possibly a comparative advantage in order to earn profits. Risk management can entail taking risk as well as reducing risk.

5. A. Assuming that the desk pays its traders a percentage of the profits on their own trading books, the −€20 million loss generated by an individual trader implies that the rest of the desk made €30 million and that the bank will have to pay the other traders an incentive fee on this larger amount, even though it generated only €10 million in net revenues. By contrast, if every trader had made money and the revenues to the desk were €10 million, the incentive payouts to traders would have been much lower and the net profits to the bank much higher.

   B. In the scenario described above, the trader in question appears to have increased his risk exposure at year-end. The asymmetric nature of the incentive fee arrangement may induce risk taking because it is a call option on a percentage of profits and the value of a call option increases in the volatility of the underlying. In this sense, the interests of the bank and the trader diverged to the detriment of the bank.

   C. First and foremost, it is clear that senior management was out of touch with the risk dynamics of the desk because it should have known that the trader in question was over his limits at some points much earlier in the scenario. The fact that management discovered this violation only after the loss occurred reflects poor risk governance.

6. *Strengths*: The sensitivity analysis reported by Ford is useful in highlighting the possible adverse effect of a 1% increase in interest rates on Ford Credit's net income. It also is based on an objective measure of interest rate risk, duration.

   Weaknesses: The sensitivity analysis reported in the table assumes that interest rate changes are instantaneous, small, parallel shifts in the yield curve. From a risk management perspective, one would have a special interest in the effects of larger interest rate changes, including major discontinuities in interest rates. The inclusion of value at risk would help fill this gap in the analysis. Furthermore, changes in the yield curve other than parallel shifts should be examined, such as nonparallel shifts (twists) in the yield curve. The text mentions the recommendation of the Derivatives Policy Group to examine both parallel shifts and twists of the yield curve.

7. A. There is a 1% chance that the portfolio will lose at least £4.25 million in any given week.

   B. There is a 99% chance that the portfolio will lose no more than £4.25 million in one week.

8. Statement A, which is the definition of VaR, is clearly correct. Statement B is also correct, because it lists the important decisions involved in measuring VaR. Statement D is correct: The longer the time period, the larger the possible losses. Statement C, however, is incorrect. The VaR number would be larger for a 1% probability than for a 5% probability. Accordingly, the correct answer is C.

9. A. The probability is 0.005 that the portfolio will lose at least 50% in a year. The probability is 0.005 that the portfolio will lose between 40% and 50% in a year. Cumulating these two probabilities implies that the probability is 0.01 that the portfolio will lose at least 40% in a year. So, the 1% yearly VaR is 40% of the market value of $10 million, which is $4 million.

   B. The probability is 0.005 that the portfolio will lose at least 50% in a year, 0.005 that it will lose between 40 and 50%, 0.010 that it will lose between 30 and 40%, 0.015 that it will lose between 20 and 30%, and 0.015 that it will lose between 10 and 20%. Cumulating these probabilities indicates that the probability is 0.05 that the portfolio will lose at least 10% in a year. So, the 5% yearly VaR is 10% of the market value of $10 million, which is $1 million.

10. First, we must calculate the monthly portfolio expected return and standard deviation. Using "1" to indicate the US government bonds and "2" to indicate the UK government bonds, we have

$$\mu_P = w_1\mu_1 + w_2\mu_2 = 0.50(0.0085) + 0.50(0.0095) = 0.0090$$

$$\sigma_P^2 = w_1^2\sigma_1^2 + w_2^2\sigma_2^2 + 2w_1 w_2 \sigma_1 \sigma_2 \rho$$
$$= (0.50)^2 (0.0320)^2 + (0.50)^2 (0.0526)^2$$
$$+ 2(0.50)(0.50)(0.0320)(0.0526)(0.35)$$
$$= 0.001242$$

$$\sigma_P = \sqrt{0.001242} = 0.0352$$

   A. For a 5% monthly VaR, we have $\mu_P - 1.65\sigma_P = 0.0090 - 1.65(0.0352) = -0.0491$. Then the VaR would be $100,000,000(0.0491) = $4.91 million.

   B. For a 1% monthly VaR, we have $\mu_P - 2.33\sigma_P = 0.0090 - 2.33(0.0352) = -0.0730$. Then the VaR would be $100,000,000(0.0730) = $7.30 million.

   C. There are 12 months or 52 weeks in a year. So, to convert the monthly return of 0.0090 to weekly return, we first multiply the monthly return by 12 to convert it to an annual return, and then we divide the annual return by 52 to convert it to a weekly return. So, the expected weekly return is $0.0090(12/52) = 0.0021$. Similarly, we adjust the standard deviation to $0.0352\left(\sqrt{12}/\sqrt{52}\right) = 0.01691$. The 5% weekly VaR would then be $\mu_P - 1.65\sigma_P = 0.0021 - 1.65(0.01691) = -0.0258$. Then the VaR in dollars would be $100,000,000(0.0258) = $2.58 million.

   D. The 1% weekly VaR would be $\mu_P - 2.33\sigma_P = 0.0021 - 2.33(0.01691) = -0.0373$. Then the VaR would be $100,000,000(0.0373) = $3.73 million.

11. A. For the five-year period, there are 60 monthly returns. Of the 60 returns, the 5% worst are the 3 worst returns. Therefore, based on the historical method, the 5% VaR would be the third worst return. From the returns given, the third worst return is −0.1980. So, the VaR in dollars is 0.1980($25,000) = $4,950.

   B. Of the 60 returns, the 1% worst are the 0.6 worst returns. Therefore, we would use the single worst return. From the returns given, the worst return is −0.2597. So, the VaR in dollars is 0.2597($25,000) = $6,492.50.

12. A. Of the 700 outcomes, the worst 5% are the 35 worst returns. Therefore, the 5% VaR would be the 35th worst return. From the data given, the 35th worst return is −0.223. So, the 5% annual VaR in dollars is 0.223($10,000,000) = $2,230,000.

    B. Of the 700 outcomes, the worst 1% are the 7 worst returns. Therefore, the 1% VaR would be the seventh worst return. From the data given, the seventh worst return is −0.347. So, the 1% annual VaR in dollars is 0.347($10,000,000) = $3,470,000.

13. A. The analytical or variance–covariance method begins with the assumption that portfolio returns are normally distributed. A normal distribution has an unlimited upside and an unlimited downside. The assumption of a normal distribution is inappropriate when the portfolio contains options because the return distributions of options are far from normal. Call options have unlimited upside potential, as in a normal distribution, but the downside return is truncated at a loss of 100%. Similarly, put options have a limited upside and a large but limited downside. Likewise, covered calls and protective puts have limits in one direction or the other. Therefore, for the portfolio that has options, the assumption of a normal distribution to estimate VaR has a number of problems. In addition, it is very difficult to calculate a covariance between either two options or an option and a security with more linear characteristics—among other reasons because options have different dynamics at different points in their life cycle.

    B. Portfolios with simple, linear characteristics, particularly those with a limited budget for computing resources and analytical personnel, might select the variance/covariance method. For more complex portfolios containing options and time-sensitive bonds, the historical method might be more appropriate. The Monte Carlo simulation method typically would not be a wise choice unless it were managed by an organization with a portfolio of complex derivatives that is willing to make and sustain a considerable investment in technology and human capital.

14. A. The observed outcomes are consistent with the VaR calculation's prediction on the frequency of losses exceeding the VaR. Therefore, the VaR calculation is accurate.

    B. The VaR results indicate that under "normal" market conditions that would characterize 19 out of 20 days, the portfolio ought to lose less than €3 million. It provides no other information beyond this.

    C. The portfolio certainly lends itself to scenario analysis. In this particular case, given the substantial short options position, it might be instructive to create a customized scenario under which the portfolio was analyzed in the wake of a large increase in option-implied volatility.

15. The fact that credit losses occur infrequently makes Statement A incorrect. Unlike a European-style option, which cannot be exercised prior to expiration and thus has no current credit risk, an American-style option does have the potential for current credit risk. Therefore, Statement C is incorrect. Statement B, however, is correct.

16. A. The decision not to hedge this risk was correct. Suppose the company had hedged this risk. If the price of oil were to increase, the favorable effect of the increase on income would be offset by the loss on the oil futures, but the home currency should appreciate against the US dollar, leaving the company worse off. If the price of oil were to decrease, the unfavorable effect on income would be offset by the futures position and the home currency should depreciate, leaving the company better off. In short, the company would remain exposed to exchange rate risk associated with oil price movements.

B. The decision not to hedge this risk was correct. The company should remain exposed to market risk associated with exchange rate movements (i.e., currency risk). Hedging would remove currency risk but leave the company with market risk associated with oil price movements. If the home currency declined, the price of oil would likely decline because it is positively correlated with the US dollar value of the home currency. That would be a negative for income. On the other hand, appreciation of the home currency is likely to be accompanied by an oil price increase, which would be positive for income.

C. The risk management strategy adopted is logical because it exploits a natural hedge. A decline in the price of oil (a negative) is likely to be accompanied by a depreciation of the home currency relative to the US dollar (a positive), and an increase in the price of oil (a positive) is likely to be accompanied by appreciation of the home currency (a negative). Hedging both currency and market risk would be an alternative risk management strategy to consider, but in comparison to the strategy adopted, it would incur transaction costs.

17. A. Because the option is a European-style option, it cannot be exercised prior to expiration. Therefore, there is no current credit risk.

B. The current value of the potential credit risk is the current market value of the option, which is $6. Of course, at expiration, the option is likely to be worth a different amount and could even expire out of the money.

C. Options have unilateral credit risk. The risk is borne by the buyer of the option, Tony Smith, because he will look to the seller for the payoff at expiration if the option expires in the money.

18. The Sharpe ratio uses standard deviation of portfolio return as the measure of risk. Standard deviation is a measure of total risk. RAROC uses capital at risk (defined in various ways) as the measure of risk. RoMAD uses maximum drawdown as a risk measure. Maximum drawdown is the difference between a portfolio's maximum point of return and the lowest point of return over a given time interval. The Sortino ratio measures risk using downside deviation, which computes volatility using only rate of return data points below a minimum acceptable return. In contrast to the Sharpe ratio, its focus is on downside risk.

19. C is correct. The monthly return is 9.6%/12 = 0.8%.
The monthly standard deviation is $18.0\%/\sqrt{12} = 5.196\%$.
The% VaR is 0.8% − 1.65 (5.196%) = −7.7734%.
The dollar VaR is 7.7734% (€50 million) = €3.8867 million, or €3.9 million.

20. B is correct. Stolz' Statement #2 is the only incorrect statement. The VaR will be larger for a 1% probability than for a 5% probability. A 1% probability is equivalent to a 99% confidence level. This requires movement 2.33 standard deviations in the direction of lower returns.

21. A is correct. Kreuzer is wrong on both. For the currency forward contract, the London securities house is bearing credit risk because the London house is the party that would be owed (or paid) at current prices. For option contracts, including puts, the option buyer is the only party with credit risk. So Kalton Corporation is bearing credit risk on its long put position.

22. A is correct. In a credit default swap, the protection seller would make payments to the protection buyer in the event of a specified credit event. Thus, the protection seller is assuming credit risk. The other positions would not give a desired increase in credit risk exposure in corporate bonds.

23. B is correct. Kreuzer's statement is incorrect with respect to the increase in expected return but correct with respect to the increased correlation. A 5% VaR would be equal to the expected monthly portfolio return minus 1.65 × (monthly portfolio standard deviation), or $-\text{VaR} = \mu_p - 1.65\sigma_p$. The increase in expected return would result in a lower calculated VaR (smaller losses). An increase in the correlation would increase the portfolio standard deviation, which would result in a higher calculated VaR (larger losses).

24. B is correct. Kreuzer's statement about an advantage of VaR is wrong because the VaR for individual positions does not generally aggregate in a simple way into portfolio VaR. The correlation of the individual positions has to be taken into account. Kreuzer's statement about the Sharpe ratio is correct.

CHAPTER 7

RISK MANAGEMENT APPLICATIONS OF FORWARD AND FUTURES STRATEGIES

SOLUTIONS

1. A. The number of futures contracts that must be bought is

$$N_f = \left(\frac{1.2 - 0.95}{0.98}\right)\left(\frac{\$175,000,000}{\$105,790}\right) = 421.99$$

Rounded off, this is 422 contracts.

B. The value of the stock portfolio is $175,000,000(1 + 0.051) = \$183,925,000$.

The profit on the long futures position is $422(\$111,500 - \$105,790) = \$2,409,620$.

The overall value of the position (stock plus long futures) is $183,925,000 + \$2,409,620 = \$186,334,620$.

$$\text{The overall rate of return is } \left(\frac{\$186,334,620}{\$175,000,000}\right) - 1 = 0.0648.$$

The effective beta is $0.0648/0.055 = 1.18$, which is approximately equal to the target beta of 1.2.

2. A. The number of futures contracts that must be bought is

$$N_f = \frac{\$300,000,000(1.0235)^{0.25}}{\$500(498.30)} = 1,211.11$$

Rounded off, this is 1,211 contracts long.

Now invest the following amount in risk-free bonds, which pay 2.35% interest:

$$\frac{1,211(\$500)(498.30)}{(1.0235)^{0.25}} = \$299,973,626$$

This amount will grow to $299,973,626(1.0235)^{0.25} = \$301,720,650$. The number of synthetic units of stock is

$$\frac{1211(500)}{(1.0075)^{0.25}} = 604,369.98$$

which would grow to $604,369.98(1.0075)^{0.25} = 605,500$ with the reinvestment of dividends.

B. At expiration in three months, the payoff on the futures is $1,211(\$500)(594.65 - 498.30) = 605,500(594.65) - \$301,720,650$. In order to settle the futures contract, the money manager will owe $\$301,720,650$. This amount can be paid off with the proceeds from the investment in risk-free bonds, leaving the money manager with 605,500 units of the stock index, each worth 594.65. This transaction achieves the desired exposure to the stock index.

3. A. In order to create a synthetic cash position, the number of futures contracts to be sold is

$$N_f = \frac{\$25,000,000(1.0275)^{4/12}}{\$250(1170.10)} = 86.24$$

Rounded off, this is 86 contracts short.

B. The effective amount of stock committed to this transaction is actually

$$\frac{86(\$250)(1170.10)}{(1.0275)^{4/12}} = \$24,930,682$$

This amount invested at the risk-free rate should grow to $\$24,930,682(1.0275)^{4/12} = \$25,157,150$, resulting in the following number of shares:

$$\frac{86(\$250)}{(1.0125)^{4/12}} = 21,411.16$$

With reinvestment of dividends, this number would grow to 21,411.16 $(1.0125)^{4/12} = 21,500$ shares. The short position in futures is equivalent to selling $\$24,930,682$ of stock.

C. In four months when the futures contract expires, the stock index is at 1031. The payoff of the futures contract is $-86(\$250)(1031 - 1170.10) = -\$21,500(1031) + \$25,157,150 = \$2,990,650$.

Netting the futures payoff against the stock position produces $\$25,157,150$, equivalent to investing $\$24,930,682$ at 2.75% for four months. The short futures position has thus effectively converted equity to cash.

4. A. The current allocation is as follows: stocks, $0.65(200,000,000) = \$130,000,000$; bonds, $0.35(\$200,000,000) = \$70,000,000$. The new allocation desired is as follows: stocks, $0.85(\$200,000,000) = \$170,000,000$; bonds, $0.15(\$200,000,000) = \$30,000,000$. So, to achieve the new allocation, the manager must buy stock futures on $\$170,000,000 - \$130,000,000 = \$40,000,000$. An equivalent amount of bond futures must be sold.

To synthetically sell $40 million in bonds and convert into cash, the manager must sell futures:

$$N_{bf} = \left(\frac{0.0 - 6.75}{5.25}\right)\left(\frac{\$40,000,000}{\$109,000}\right) = -471.82$$

He should sell 472 contracts and create synthetic cash.

To synthetically buy $40 million of stock with synthetic cash, the manager must buy futures:

$$N_{sf} = \left(\frac{1.15-0}{0.95}\right)\left(\frac{\$40,000,000}{\$157,500}\right) = 307.44$$

He should buy 307 contracts. Now the manager effectively has $170 million (85%) in stocks and $30 million (15%) in bonds.

The next step is to increase the beta on the $170 million in stock to 1.20 by purchasing futures. The number of futures contracts would, therefore, be

$$N_{sf} = \left(\frac{1.20-1.15}{0.95}\right)\left(\frac{\$170,000,000}{\$157,500}\right) = 56.81$$

An additional 57 stock futures contracts should be purchased. In total, $307 + 57 = 364$ contracts are bought.

To increase the modified duration from 6.75 to 8.25 on the $30 million of bonds, the number of futures contracts is

$$N_{bf} = \left(\frac{8.25-6.75}{5.25}\right)\left(\frac{\$30,000,000}{\$109,000}\right) = 78.64$$

An additional 79 bond futures contracts should be purchased. In total, $472 - 79 = 393$ contracts are sold.

B. The value of the stock will be $130,000,000(1 + 0.05) = \$136,500,000$. The profit on the stock index futures will be $364(\$164,005 - \$157,500) = \$2,367,820$.

The value of the bonds will be $70,000,000(1 + 0.0135) = \$70,945,000$. The profit on the bond futures will be $-393(\$110,145 - \$109,000) = -\$449,985$.

The total value of the position, therefore, is $\$136,500,000 + \$2,367,820 + \$70,945,000 - \$449,985 = \$209,362,835$.

If the reallocation were carried out by trading bonds and stocks: The stock would be worth $\$170,000,000(1 + 0.05) = \$178,500,000$. The bonds would be worth $\$30,000,000(1 + 0.0135) = \$30,405,000$. The overall value of the portfolio would be $\$178,500,000 + \$30,405,000 = \$208,905,000$.

The difference between the two approaches is $457,835, only 0.229% of the original value of the portfolio.

5. A. In order to gain effective exposure to stock and bonds today, the manager must use futures to synthetically buy $17,500,000 of stock and $32,500,000 of bonds.

To synthetically buy $17,500,000 in stock, the manager must buy futures:

$$N_{sf} = \left(\frac{1.15-0}{0.93}\right)\left(\frac{\$17,500,000}{\$175,210}\right) = 123.51$$

He should buy 124 contracts.

To synthetically buy $32,500,000 of bonds, the manager must buy futures:

$$N_{bf} = \left(\frac{7.65-0}{5.65}\right)\left(\frac{\$32,500,000}{\$95,750}\right) = 459.57$$

He should buy 460 contracts.

Now the manager effectively has invested $17,500,000 in stock and $32,500,000 in bonds.

B. The profit on the stock index futures will be $124(\$167,559 - \$175,210) = -\$948,724$.
   The profit on the bond futures will be $460(\$93,586 - \$95,750) = -\$995,440$.
   The total profit with futures = $-\$948,724 - \$995,440 = -\$1,944,164$.
   If bonds and stocks were purchased today, in three months:

   The change in value of stock would be $\$17,500,000(-0.054) = -\$945,000$.
   The change in value of bonds would be $\$32,500,000(-0.0306) = -\$994,500$.

   The overall change in value of the portfolio would be $-\$945,000 - \$994,500 = -\$1,939,500$.
   The difference between the two approaches is $4,664, only 0.009% of the total expected cash inflow.

6. A. GateCorp will receive £200,000,000 in two months. To hedge the risk that the pound may weaken during this period, the firm should enter into a forward contract to deliver pounds and receive dollars two months from now at a price fixed now. Because it is effectively long the pound, GateCorp will take a short position on the pound in the forward market. GateCorp will thus enter into a two-month short forward contract to deliver £200,000,000 at a rate of $1.4272 per pound.

   When the forward contract expires in two months, irrespective of the spot exchange rate, GateCorp will deliver £200,000,000 and receive $(\$1.4272/£1)$ $(£200,000,000) = \$285,440,000$.

B. ABCorp will have to pay A$175,000,000 in one month. To hedge the risk that the Australian dollar may strengthen against the US dollar during this period, it should enter into a forward contract to purchase Australian dollars one month from now at a price fixed today. Because it is effectively short the Australian dollar, ABCorp takes a long position in the forward market. ABCorp thus enters into a one-month long forward contract to purchase A$175,000,000 at a rate of US$0.5249 per Australian dollar.

   When the forward contract expires in one month, irrespective of the spot exchange rate, ABCorp will pay $(\$0.5249/A\$)(A\$175,000,000) = \$91,857,500$ to purchase A$175,000,000. This amount is used to purchase the raw material needed.

CHAPTER 8

RISK MANAGEMENT APPLICATIONS OF OPTION STRATEGIES

SOLUTIONS

1. A. This position is commonly called a bull spread.
    B. Let X_1 be the lower of the two strike prices and X_2 be the higher of the two strike prices.

    i. $V_T = \max(0, S_T - X_1) - \max(0, S_T - X_2)$
        $= \max(0, 89 - 75) - \max(0, 89 - 85) = 14 - 4 = 10$
        $\Pi = V_T - V_0 = V_T - (c_1 - c_2) = 10 - (10 - 2) = 2$

    ii. $V_T = \max(0, S_T - X_1) - \max(0, S_T - X_2)$
        $= \max(0, 78 - 75) - \max(0, 78 - 85) = 3 - 0 = 3$
        $\Pi = V_T - V_0 = V_T - (c_1 - c_2) = 3 - (10 - 2) = -5$

    iii. $V_T = \max(0, S_T - X_1) - \max(0, S_T - X_2)$
        $= \max(0, 70 - 75) - \max(0, 70 - 85) = 0 - 0 = 0$
        $\Pi = V_T - V_0 = V_T - (c_1 - c_2) = 0 - (10 - 2) = -8$

    C. i. Maximum profit $= X_2 - X_1 - (c_1 - c_2) = 85 - 75 - (10 - 2) = 2$
        ii. Maximum loss $= c_1 - c_2 = 10 - 2 = 8$
    D. $S_T^* = X_1 + (c_1 - c_2) = 75 + (10 - 2) = 83$
    E. $V_T = \max(0, S_T - X_1) - \max(0, S_T - X_2)$
        $= \max(0, 83 - 75) - \max(0, 83 - 85) = 8 - 0 = 8$
        $\Pi = V_T - V_0 = V_T - (c_1 - c_2) = 8 - (10 - 2) = 0$

Therefore, the profit or loss if the price of the underlying increases to 83 at expiration is indeed zero.

2. A. This position is commonly called a bear spread.

   B. Let X_1 be the lower of the two strike prices and X_2 be the higher of the two strike prices.

   i. $V_T = \max(0, X_2 - S_T) - \max(0, X_1 - S_T)$
      $= \max(0, 0.85 - 0.87) - \max(0, 0.70 - 0.87) = 0 - 0 = 0$
      $\Pi = V_T - V_0 = V_T - (p_2 - p_1) = 0 - (0.15 - 0.03) = -0.12$

   ii. $V_T = \max(0, X_2 - S_T) - \max(0, X_1 - S_T)$
       $= \max(0, 0.85 - 0.78) - \max(0, 0.70 - 0.78) = 0.07 - 0 = 0.07$
       $\Pi = V_T - V_0 = V_T - (p_2 - p_1) = 0.07 - (0.15 - 0.03) = -0.05$

   iii. $V_T = \max(0, X_2 - S_T) - \max(0, X_1 - S_T)$
        $= \max(0, 0.85 - 0.68) - \max(0, 0.70 - 0.68) = 0.17 - 0.02 = 0.15$
        $\Pi = V_T - V_0 = V_T - (p_2 - p_1) = 0.15 - (0.15 - 0.03) = 0.03$

   C. i. Maximum profit $= X_2 - X_1 - (p_2 - p_1)$
         $= 0.85 - 0.70 - (0.15 - 0.03) = 0.03$

      ii. Maximum loss $= p_2 - p_1 = 0.15 - 0.03 = 0.12$

   D. Breakeven point $= X_2 - (p_2 - p_1) = 0.85 - (0.15 - 0.03) = 0.73$

   E. $V_T = \max(0, X_2 - S_T) - \max(0, X_1 - S_T)$
      $= \max(0, 0.85 - 0.73) - \max(0, 0.70 - 0.73) = 0.12 - 0 = 0.12$
      $\Pi = V_T - V_0 = V_T - (p_2 - p_1) = 0.12 - (0.15 - 0.03) = 0$

   Therefore, the profit or loss if the price of the currency decreases to $0.73 at expiration of the puts is indeed zero.

3. A. Let X_1 be 110, X_2 be 115, and X_3 be 120.

   $$V_0 = c_1 - 2c_2 + c_3 = 8 - 2(5) + 3 = 1$$

   i. $V_T = \max(0, S_T - X_1) - 2\max(0, S_T - X_2) + \max(0, S_T - X_3)$
      $V_T = \max(0, 106 - 110) - 2\max(0, 106 - 115)$
      $\quad + \max(0, 106 - 120) = 0$
      $\Pi = V_T - V_0 = 0 - 1 = -1$

   ii. $V_T = \max(0, S_T - X_1) - 2\max(0, S_T - X_2) + \max(0, S_T - X_3)$
       $V_T = \max(0, 110 - 110) - 2\max(0, 110 - 115)$
       $\quad + \max(0, 110 - 120) = 0$
       $\Pi = V_T - V_0 = 0 - 1 = -1$

   iii. $V_T = \max(0, S_T - X_1) - 2\max(0, S_T - X_2) + \max(0, S_T - X_3)$
        $V_T = \max(0, 115 - 110) - 2\max(0, 115 - 115)$
        $\quad + \max(0, 115 - 120) = 5$
        $\Pi = V_T - V_0 = 5 - 1 = 4$

iv. $V_T = \max(0, S_T - X_1) - 2\max(0, S_T - X_2) + \max(0, S_T - X_3)$
$V_T = \max(0, 120 - 110) - 2\max(0, 120 - 115)$
$\qquad + \max(0, 120 - 120) = 10 - 10 + 0 = 0$
$\Pi = V_T - V_0 = 0 - 1 = -1$

v. $V_T = \max(0, S_T - X_1) - 2\max(0, S_T - X_2) + \max(0, S_T - X_3)$
$V_T = \max(0, 123 - 110) - 2\max(0, 123 - 115)$
$\qquad + \max(0, 123 - 120) = 13 - 16 + 3 = 0$
$\Pi = V_T - V_0 = 0 - 1 = -1$

B. i. Maximum profit = $X_2 - X_1 - (c_1 - 2c_2 + c_3) = 115 - 110 - 1 = 4$

ii. Maximum loss = $c_1 - 2c_2 + c_3 = 1$

iii. The maximum profit would be realized if the price of the stock at expiration of the options is at the exercise price of \$115.

iv. The maximum loss would be incurred if the price of the stock is at or below the exercise price of \$110, or if the price of the stock is at or above the exercise price of \$120.

C. Breakeven: $S_T{}^* = X_1 + (c_1 - 2c_2 + c_3)$ and $S_T{}^* = 2X_2 - X_1 - (c_1 - 2c_2 + c_3)$.
So, $S_T{}^* = 110 + 1 = 111$ and $S_T{}^* = 2(115) - 110 - 1 = 119$

4. A. Let X_1 be 110, X_2 be 115, and X_3 be 120.

$$V_0 = p_1 - 2p_2 + p_3 = 3.50 - 2(6) + 9 = 0.50$$

i. $V_T = \max(0, X_1 - S_T) - 2\max(0, X_2 - S_T) + \max(0, X_3 - S_T)$
$V_T = \max(0, 110 - 106) - 2\max(0, 115 - 106)$
$\qquad + \max(0, 120 - 106) = 4 - 2(9) + 14 = 0$
$\Pi = V_T - V_0 = 0 - 0.50 = -0.50$

ii. $V_T = \max(0, X_1 - S_T) - 2\max(0, X_2 - S_T) + \max(0, X_3 - S_T)$
$V_T = \max(0, 110 - 110) - 2\max(0, 115 - 110)$
$\qquad + \max(0, 120 - 110) = 0 - 2(5) + 10 = 0$
$\Pi = V_T - V_0 = 0 - 0.50 = -0.50$

iii. $V_T = \max(0, X_1 - S_T) - 2\max(0, X_2 - S_T) + \max(0, X_3 - S_T)$
$V_T = \max(0, 110 - 115) - 2\max(0, 115 - 115)$
$\qquad + \max(0, 120 - 115) = 0 - 2(0) + 5 = 5$
$\Pi = V_T - V_0 = 5 - 0.50 = 4.50$

iv. $V_T = \max(0, X_1 - S_T) - 2\max(0, X_2 - S_T) + \max(0, X_3 - S_T)$
$V_T = \max(0, 110 - 120) - 2\max(0, 115 - 120)$
$\qquad + \max(0, 120 - 120) = 0$
$\Pi = V_T - V_0 = 0 - 0.50 = -0.50$

v. $V_T = \max(0, X_1 - S_T) - 2\max(0, X_2 - S_T) + \max(0, X_3 - S_T)$
$V_T = \max(0, 110 - 123) - 2\max(0, 115 - 123)$
$\qquad + \max(0, 120 - 123) = 0$
$\Pi = V_T - V_0 = 0 - 0.50 = -0.50$

B.   i. Maximum profit $= X_2 - X_1 - (p_1 - 2p_2 + p_3) = 115 - 110 - 0.50 = 4.50$

    ii. Maximum loss $= p_1 - 2p_2 + p_3 = 0.50$

    iii. The maximum profit would be realized if the expiration price of the stock is at the exercise price of \$115.

    iv. The maximum loss would be incurred if the expiration price of the stock is at or below the exercise price of \$110, or if the expiration price of the stock is at or above the exercise price of \$120.

C. Breakeven: $S_T^* = X_1 + (p_1 - 2p_2 + p_3)$ and $S_T^* = 2X_2 - X_1 - (p_1 - 2p_2 + p_3)$.

So, $S_T^* = 110 + 0.50 = 110.50$ and $S_T^* = 2(115) - 110 - 0.50 = 119.50$.

D. For $S_T = 110.50$:

$$V_T = \max(0, X_1 - S_T) - 2\max(0, X_2 - S_T) + \max(0, X_3 - S_T)$$
$$V_T = \max(0, 110 - 110.50) - 2\max(0, 115 - 110.50) + \max(0, 120 - 110.50)$$
$$= -2(4.50) + 9.50 = 0.50$$
$$\Pi = V_T - V_0 = 0.50 - 0.50 = 0$$

For $S_T = 119.50$:

$$V_T = \max(0, X_1 - S_T) - 2\max(0, X_2 - S_T) + \max(0, X_3 - S_T)$$
$$V_T = \max(0, 110 - 119.50) - 2\max(0, 115 - 119.50) + \max(0, 120 - 119.50) = 0.50$$
$$\Pi = V_T - V_0 = 0.50 - 0.50 = 0$$

Therefore, we see that the profit or loss at the breakeven points computed in Part D above is indeed zero.

5. A.   i. $V_T = S_T + \max(0, X_1 - S_T) - \max(0, S_T - X_2)$

      $= 92 + \max(0, 75 - 92) - \max(0, 92 - 90) = 92 + 0 - 2 = 90$

      $\Pi = V_T - S_0 = 90 - 80 = 10$

    ii. $V_T = S_T + \max(0, X_1 - S_T) - \max(0, S_T - X_2)$

      $= 90 + \max(0, 75 - 90) - \max(0, 90 - 90) = 90 + 0 - 0 = 90$

      $\Pi = V_T - S_0 = 90 - 80 = 10$

    iii. $V_T = S_T + \max(0, X_1 - S_T) - \max(0, S_T - X_2)$

      $= 82 + \max(0, 75 - 82) - \max(0, 82 - 90) = 82 + 0 - 0 = 82$

      $\Pi = V_T - S_0 = 82 - 80 = 2$

    iv. $V_T = S_T + \max(0, X_1 - S_T) - \max(0, S_T - X_2)$

      $= 75 + \max(0, 75 - 75) - \max(0, 75 - 90) = 75 + 0 - 0 = 75$

      $\Pi = V_T - S_0 = 75 - 80 = -5$

    v. $V_T = S_T + \max(0, X_1 - S_T) - \max(0, S_T - X_2)$

      $= 70 + \max(0, 75 - 70) - \max(0, 70 - 90) = 70 + 5 - 0 = 75$

      $\Pi = V_T - S_0 = 75 - 80 = -5$

B.   i. Maximum profit $= X_2 - S_0 = 90 - 80 = 10$

    ii. Maximum loss $= -(X_1 - S_0) = -(75 - 80) = 5$

    iii. The maximum profit would be realized if the price of the stock at the expiration of options is at or above the exercise price of \$90.

    iv. The maximum loss would be incurred if the price of the stock at the expiration of options was at or below the exercise price of \$75.

C. Breakeven: $S_T^* = S_0 = 80$

6. A. This position is commonly called a straddle.

B. i. $V_T = \max(0, S_T - X) + \max(0, X - S_T)$
$= \max(0, 35 - 25) + \max(0, 25 - 35) = 10 + 0 = 10$
$\Pi = V_T - (c_0 + p_0) = 10 - (4 + 1) = 5$

ii. $V_T = \max(0, S_T - X) + \max(0, X - S_T)$
$= \max(0, 29 - 25) + \max(0, 25 - 29) = 4 + 0 = 4$
$\Pi = V_T - (c_0 + p_0) = 4 - (4 + 1) = -1$

iii. $V_T = \max(0, S_T - X) + \max(0, X - S_T)$
$= \max(0, 25 - 25) + \max(0, 25 - 25) = 0 + 0 = 0$
$\Pi = V_T - (c_0 + p_0) = 0 - (4 + 1) = -5$

iv. $V_T = \max(0, S_T - X) + \max(0, X - S_T)$
$= \max(0, 20 - 25) + \max(0, 25 - 20) = 0 + 5 = 5$
$\Pi = V_T - (c_0 + p_0) = 5 - (4 + 1) = 0$

v. $V_T = \max(0, S_T - X) + \max(0, X - S_T)$
$= \max(0, 15 - 25) + \max(0, 25 - 15) = 0 + 10 = 10$
$\Pi = V_T - (c_0 + p_0) = 10 - (4 + 1) = 5$

C. i. Maximum profit $= \infty$
ii. Maximum loss $= c_0 + p_0 = 4 + 1 = 5$
D. $S_T^* = X \pm (c_0 + p_0) = 25 \pm (4 + 1) = 30, 20$

7. C is correct. A protective put accomplishes Hopewell's goal of short-term price protection. A protective put provides downside protection while retaining the upside potential. While Hopewell is concerned about the downside in the short-term, he wants to remain invested in Walnut shares, as he is positive about the stock in the long-term.

8. A is correct. The straddle strategy is a strategy based upon the expectation of high volatility in the underlying stock. The straddle strategy consists of simultaneously buying a call option and a put option at the same strike price. Singh could recommend that French buy a straddle using near at-the-money options ($67.50 strike). This allows French to profit should Walnut stock price experience a large move in either direction after the earnings release.

9. A is correct. The straddle strategy consists of simultaneously buying a call option and buying a put option at the same strike price. The market price for the $67.50 call option is $1.99, and the market price for the $67.50 put option is $2.26, for an initial net cost of $4.25 per share. Thus, this straddle position requires a move greater than $4.25 in either direction from the strike price of $67.50 to become profitable. So, the straddle becomes profitable at $67.50 − $4.26 = $63.24 or lower, or $67.50 + $4.26 = $71.76 or higher. At $63.24, the profit on the straddle is positive.

10. A is correct. The bull call strategy consists of buying the lower strike option, and selling the higher strike option. The purchase of the $65 strike call option costs $3.65 per share, and selling the $70 strike call option generates an inflow of $0.91 per share, for an initial net cost of $2.74 per share. At expiration, the maximum profit occurs when the stock price is $70 or higher, which yields a $5.00 per share payoff ($70 − 65). After deduction of the $2.74 per share cost required to initiate the bull call spread, the profit is $2.26 ($5.00 − $2.74).

11. B is correct. The butterfly strategy consists of buying a call option with a low strike price ($65), selling 2 call options with a higher strike price ($67.50), and buying another call option with an even higher strike price ($70). The market price for the $65 call option is $3.65 per share, the market price for the $70 call option is $0.91 per share, and selling the two call options generates an inflow of $3.98 per share (market price of $1.99 per share x 2 contracts). Thus, the initial net cost of the butterfly position is $3.65 + $0.91 − $3.98 = $0.58 per share. If Walnut shares are $66 at expiration, the $67.50 strike option and $70 strike option are both out-of-the-money and therefore worthless. The $65 call option is in the money by $1.00 per share, and after deducting the cost of $0.58 per share to initiate the butterfly position, the net profit is $0.42 per share.

12. B is correct. The $67.50 call option is approximately at-the-money, as Walnut share price is currently $67.76. A gamma measures i) the deviation of the exact option price changes from the price change approximated by the delta and ii) the sensitivity of delta to a change in the underlying. The largest moves for gamma occur when options are trading at-the-money or near expiration, when the deltas of at-the-money options move quickly toward 1.0 or 0.0. Under these conditions, the gammas tend to be largest and delta hedges are hardest to maintain.

CHAPTER 9

RISK MANAGEMENT APPLICATIONS OF SWAP STRATEGIES

SOLUTIONS

1. The company can enter into a swap to pay a fixed rate of 6.5% and receive a floating rate. The first floating payment will be at 5%.

   Interest payment on the floating rate note = $50,000,000(0.05 + 0.0125)(90/360) = $781,250
   Swap fixed payment = $50,000,000(0.065)(90/360) = $812,500
   Swap floating receipts = $50,000,000(0.05)(90/360) = $625,000

   The overall cash payment made by the company is $812,500 + $781,250 − $625,000 = $968,750.

2. A. The value of the bond portfolio is inversely related to interest rates. To increase the duration, it would be necessary to hold a position that moves inversely with the interest rates. Hence the swap should be pay floating, receive fixed.

   B. Duration of a four-year pay-floating, receive-fixed swap with quarterly payments = $(0.75)(4) − 0.125 = 2.875$

      Duration of a three-year pay-floating, receive-fixed swap with semiannual payments = $(0.75)(3) − 0.25 = 2.0$

      Because the objective is to increase the duration of the bond portfolio, the four-year pay-floating, receive-fixed swap is the better choice.

   C. The notional principal is

$$NP = B\left(\frac{MDUR_T - MDUR_B}{MDUR_S}\right)$$

$$NP = \$100,000,000\left(\frac{3.5 - 1.5}{2.875}\right) = \$69,565,217$$

3. Because the company has a floating-rate obligation on the floating-rate note, it should enter into a swap that involves receiving a floating rate. Accordingly, the appropriate swap to hedge the risk and earn a profit would be a pay-fixed, receive-floating swap. Let Libor be L. Cash flows generated at each step are as follows:

A. Issue leveraged floating-rate notes and pay coupon =
$L(2.5)(\$5,000,000) = \$12,500,000L$

B. Buy bonds with a face value = $(2.5)(\$5,000,000) = \$12,500,000$
Receive a coupon = $(0.07)(\$12,500,000) = \$875,000$

C. Enter into a pay-fixed, receive-floating swap:

Pay = $(0.06)(2.5)(\$5,000,000) = \$750,000$
Receive = $L(2.5)(\$5,000,000) = \$12,500,000L$

D. Net cash flow = $-\$12,500,000L + \$875,000 - \$750,000 + \$12,500,000L = \$125,000$

In addition to the risk of default by the bond issuer, the company is taking the credit risk of the dealer by entering into a swap. The profit of $125,000 may be compensation for taking on this additional risk.

4. A. The US company would pay the interest rate in euros. Because it expects that the interest rate in the eurozone will fall in the future, it should choose a swap with a floating rate on the interest paid in euros to let the interest rate on its debt float down.

B. The US company would receive the interest rate in dollars. Because it expects that the interest rate in the United States will fall in the future, it should choose a swap with a fixed rate on the interest received in dollars to prevent the interest rate it receives from going down.

5. A. The semiannual cash flow that must be converted into pounds is €15,000,000/2 = €7,500,000. In order to create a swap to convert €7,500,000, the equivalent notional principals are:
   - Euro notional principal = €7,500,000/(0.065/2) = €230,769,231
   - Pound notional principal = €230,769,231/€1.5/£ = £153,846,154

B. The cash flows from the swap will now be:
   - Company makes swap payment = €230,769,231(0.065/2) = €7,500,000
   - Company receives swap payment = £153,846,154(0.075/2) = £5,769,231
   The company has effectively converted euro cash receipts to pounds.

6. A. The portfolio manager can reduce exposure to JK stock by entering into an equity swap in which the manager:
   - pays or sells the return on $30,000,000 of JK stock.
   - receives or buys the return on $30,000,000 worth of the S&P 500.

B. On the equity swap, at the end of each year, the manager will:

Pay $(0.04)(\$30,000,000) = \$1,200,000$
Receive $(-0.03)(\$30,000,000) = -\$900,000$

(Note: Receiving a negative value means paying.)

Net cash flow = $-\$1,200,000 - \$900,000 = -\$2,100,000$

Notice here that because the return on the index is significantly lower than the return on the stock, the swap has created a large cash flow problem.

7. A. The manager needs to reduce the allocation to domestic stocks by 10% and increase the allocation to international stocks by 10%. So the manager needs to reduce the allocation to domestic stocks by $(0.10)(\$750,000,000) = \$75,000,000$ and increase

the allocation to international stocks by $75,000,000. This can be done by entering into an equity swap in which the manager:

- pays or sells the return on the Russell 3000 on notional principal of $75,000,000.
- receives or buys the return on the MSCI EAFE index on notional principal of $75,000,000.

B. On the equity swap, at the end of the first year, the manager will:

Pay (0.05)($75,000,000) = $3,750,000
Receive (0.06)($75,000,000) = $4,500,000
Net cash flow = −$3,750,000 + $4,500,000 = $750,000

8. The following are the current allocations, the desired new allocations, and the transactions needed to go from the current positions to the new positions.

Stock	Current ($640 Million, 80%)	New ($600 Million, 75%)	Transaction
Large cap	$448 million (70%)	$450 million (75%)	Buy $2 million
International	$192 million (30%)	$150 million (25%)	Sell $42 million

Bonds	Current ($160 Million, 20%)	New ($200 Million, 25%)	Transaction
Government	$128 million (80%)	$150 million (75%)	Buy $22 million
Corporate	$ 32 million (20%)	$ 50 million (25%)	Buy $18 million

The following swap transactions would achieve the desired allocations:

Equity Swaps

Receive return on US large-cap index on $2,000,000
Pay Libor on $2,000,000
Pay return on international stock index on $42,000,000
Receive Libor on $42,000,000

Fixed-Income Swaps

Receive return on US government bond index on $22,000,000
Pay Libor on $22,000,000
Receive return on US corporate bond index on $18,000,000
Pay Libor on $18,000,000

The overall position involves no Libor payments or receipts. The portfolio receives Libor on $42 million on equity swaps. It pays Libor on $2 million on equity swaps, and $22 million and $18 million on fixed-income swaps, for a total payment of Libor on $42 million. Thus, overall, there are no Libor payments or receipts.

9. A. If FS(2,5) is above the exercise rate, it will be worth exercising the swaption to enter a three-year swap to pay a fixed rate of 5% and receive Libor of 6.5%.

Swap payments on first quarterly settlement date:

Pay $20,000,000(90/360)(0.05) = $250,000
Receive $20,000,000(90/360)(0.065) = $325,000
Loan payment = $20,000,000(90/360)(0.065) = $325,000

Net cash flow = −$250,000

B. If FS(2,5) is below the exercise rate, it will not be worth exercising the swaption. However, the company can enter a three-year swap to pay a fixed rate of 4%, for example, and receive Libor of 6.5%.

Swap payments on first quarterly settlement date:

Pay $20,000,000(90/360)(0.04) = $200,000
Receive $20,000,000(90/360)(0.065) = $325,000
Loan payment = $20,000,000(90/360)(0.065) = $325,000

Net cash flow = −$200,000

10. B is correct. Gide will invest the 65 billion yen for six months at 0.066% (refer to Exhibit 1). She will convert the yen to euros using the 6-month forward rate of 132.46. Solve 65,000,000,000 × [1 + (0.00066 × (180/360))]/132.46 = 490,876,114.

11. B is correct. Assuming that interest parity holds, if Gide uses a six-month forward to convert the yen, she should expect to earn the six-month euro rate of 2.13% as shown in Exhibit 1. As a check, you can convert 65 billion yen to euros at the spot exchange rate. Then, calculate the return associated with this number and the answer in the previous question. Converting at the spot gives 65,000,000,000/133.83 = 485,690,802. According to the previous question she actually ended up with 490,876,114. The return is (490,876,114 − 485,690,802)/485,690,802 = 0.01067616. Annualizing this six-month HPR provides the answer of 2.13%.

12. A is correct. Darc's statement in concern #3 describes buying a straddle. A long straddle is one way to profit from an increase in volatility as the increase in volatility will, ceteris paribus, increase the values of both the put and the call.

13. B is correct. In order to raise 100 million Swiss francs, Millau needs to issue bonds totaling 100,000,000 SF/1.554 = €64,350,064. To convert the euros into Swiss francs, Millau could enter into a currency swap. In a currency swap, notional amounts are exchanged at initiation. In this case, Millau will pay €64,350,064 and receive 100 million in Swiss francs. Subsequent payments do not net as they are denominated in different currencies. Remembering to adjust the given swap rates for semi-annual payments, in six months Millau will pay (0.008/2) × 100,000,000 = 400,000 Swiss francs and receive 64,350,064 × (0.023/2) = 740,026 euros.

14. B is correct. Darc expects interest rates in the euro zone and in Switzerland to increase. Given such an expectation, the best swap would be to pay fixed and receive floating. If the expected increases come about, the amount paid remains fixed while the amount received increases.

15. C is correct. If the stock price at expiration of the options is $26.90, the put will expire worthless, the call will expire worthless, and the value of the strategy will reflect solely the value of the stock.

16. A is correct. The protective put combines a long stock position with a long put position. The stock price of $26.20 plus the cost of the put, $0.80, provides the breakeven point for the combination, which is $27.00. If the stock price declines below $25.00, the value of the put at expiration will increase dollar-for-dollar with the stock decline. Thus, Cassidy effectively locks in a sales price of at least $25.00. At that $25.00 stock price, Cassidy loses $1.20 per share on his stock as well as the $0.80 put premium. Thus, his maximum loss is $2.00. Regarding the Sure covered call, if the Sure stock price increases above $35.00, the value of the call at expiration will increase dollar-for-dollar with increases in the share price. As Cassidy is short the call, this represents a dollar-for-dollar loss to him. Thus, the maximum gain of the covered call is the difference between today's stock price and the strike ($1.00) plus the premium received ($1.20) equals $2.20. If the stock price falls, the $1.20 premium offsets, in part, the loss. At $32.80, the $1.20 premium exactly offsets the loss on the stock. Thus, $32.80 is the breakeven point for the strategy.

17. A is correct. A protective put combines a long stock position with a long put. The put effectively "clips" the downside risk of the stock while allowing upside potential. A long call also exhibits a truncated downside and upside potential.

18. C is correct. Initially, the dealer will be long the call. Long calls have positive deltas. If stock prices fall, the value of the call will decrease, harming the dealer. To hedge the risk of a price decline, the dealer will sell the underlying.

19. B is correct. Multiply 250,000 shares times the price per share of Hop: 250,000 × $26.20 = $6,550,000. Multiply 200,000 shares times the price per share of Sure: 200,000 × $34.00 = $6,800,000. The total notional value of the swap is the sum of these two amounts: $6,550,000 + $6,800,000 = $13,350,000. If Hop is up 2%, Sure is up 4%, and the Russell 3000 is up 5%, the swap cash flows will be 0.02 × $6,550,000 plus 0.04 × $6,800,000 equals $403,000 from Eldridge to the dealer and 0.05 × $13,350,000 = $667,500 from the dealer to Eldridge. Only the net payment, $264,500 from the dealer to Cassidy, is actually paid.

20. B is correct. The target beta is 0.80 and the dollar value of the portfolio is $13,350,000. Multiply 0.80 × $13,350,000 = $10,680,000. This is the desired result. Currently, the beta of the portfolio is 1.20. Multiplying the current beta by the portfolio value generates a value of $16,020,000 (1.20 × $13,350,000). The short futures position must reduce the beta-times-dollar amount by $5,340,000 ($16,020,000 − $10,680,000). Given that the beta of the futures contract is 0.97, the dollar amount of futures contracts needed is $5,505,155 ($5,340,000/0.97). Divide this number by the per contract value of the futures contract to calculate the needed number of contracts: $5,505,155/$275,000 = 20.018 contracts. Round to 20 contracts.

21. B is correct. 20% of the $600 million equity portfolio is $120 million, and 80% is $480 million. WMTC needs to reduce its WMTC equity holding from it current value of $400 million to $120 million, a decrease of $280 million. This result implies an increase of $320 million in diversified equities. Hence, WMTC needs to pay a return on $280 million of WMTC equity and receive a return on $280 million of the S&P 500 index, which is a proxy for diversified equities.

22. A is correct. To achieve the lower target duration using an interest rate swap, Lopez needs to use an interest rate swap that has a negative modified duration, which requires a pay fixed, receive floating swap. The pay-fixed, receive-floating swap has a negative duration, because the duration of a fixed-rate bond is positive and larger than the duration of a floating-rate bond, which is near zero.

23. B is correct. Lopez would like to reduce the duration of the bond portfolio by 50% from 6 years to 3 years. The notional principal of the swap is calculated as:

[$500,000,000 × (6)] + [notional principal × (MDUR$_s$)] = [$500,000,000 × (3)]

Solving for notional principal:

$$\text{Notional Principal} = \$500,000,000 \times (3 - 6\ /\ \text{MDUR}_s)$$

To estimate the modified duration of the swap (MDUR$_s$), note that the swap's floating-rate payments are semiannual payments, which implies an average duration of 0.25 years. So, given Lopez's estimate of the duration of the swap's fixed payments to be 75% of the swap maturity, the modified duration of the swap (MDUR$_s$) is −4.25 years, calculated as:

$$0.25 - (0.75 \times 6) = -4.25 \text{ years};$$

Solving for notional principal:

$$\text{Notional principal} = \$500,000,000 \times [(3 - 6)\ /-4.25] = \$352,941,177, \text{ or}$$
$$\$353 \text{ million.}$$

24. B is correct. WMTC would enter the interest rate swap as the pay-fixed, receive-floating party, and the net interest payment would be $400,000. This net interest payment is calculated as:

    First, the loan interest payment that WMTC owes on the loan would be calculated as:

    Libor of 5% + 200 basis points = 7%

    $10,000,000 × (0.07 / 2) = $350,000.

    On the swap, the company pays a fixed rate of 6%: $10,000,000 (0.06 / 2) = $300,000, and receives a floating payment equal to Libor: $10,000,000 (0.05 / 2) = $250,000.

    So, the net interest payment would be: $250,000 − $350,000 − $300,000 = −$400,000, implying a net payment of $400,000.

25. C is correct. The notional principals for the swap, based upon the prevailing given rates, are calculated as:

    WMTC receives €6 million from Spanish operations semiannually.

    To make a swap payment equal to €6 million at the given 4.5% Euro fixed rate, the Euro notional principal would need to be €266,666,667, calculated as:

    €6 million / (0.045 / 2) = €266,666,667.

    Consequently, at the given spot rate of 1.4 USD/EUR, the USD notional principal would be $373,333,333. The given fixed rate in the US is 5%.

    So, WMTC would make a swap payment in Euros equal to €266,666,666 × 0.0225 = €6 million and receive a swap payment in US dollars of $373,333,333 × 0.025 = $9,333,333, or approximately $9.3 million.

26. B is correct. The buyer of a payer swaption holds the right to become the pay-fixed, receive-floating party in an interest rate swap. This arrangement would allow WMTC to hedge unknown Libor in two years when WMTC will need to borrow to fund the expansion.